PENGUIN BOOKS

GW00600666

party food
bible

party food
bible

Margaret Barca

contents

introduction

Whatever type of party you're having – a casual barbecue or drinks in the garden, a refined, candle-lit cocktail party or a buffet spread – the best way to enjoy it is to be organised and have a plan. You can then choose the type and quantity of food – and everything else – to match. You might decide on robust flavours, colourful bowls, chunky glassware and brightly coloured napkins, or irresistible morsels beautifully arranged on elegant platters with sparkling stemware, or a generous spread for guests to help themselves.

Make sure its achievable: you don't want to spend the entire party tied to the kitchen) but you *do* want to spoil your guests.

party food basics

Most parties are about sharing a special occasion with friends or family. Of course, food is important – in fact, food and drink and the atmosphere are all part of the mix, but no one enjoys seeing the host so overwhelmed that they can't enjoy their own party.

planning

When it comes to planning, I have three words for you – lists, lists, lists.

Write a guest list, a menu, a drinks list, a shopping list of things you can buy ahead and a list of last-minute buys, a list of any special equipment needed, a list of what to do ahead of time and what to do just before the guests arrive, a list of the order in which you will be serving food, and a list of who will be helping with the clean-up.

how much food?

If you are serving finger food, work it out as pieces per head, taking into account the time of day and the length of the party. If it is at a mealtime (say 7.30 – 9.30 p.m.) people will be hungrier and expecting more food. If your party starts after 8 p.m., guests will probably have eaten but may be hungry again later, so you can serve food a little further into the evening.

On average allow 5 pieces of finger food per person per hour for the first two hours and 3–4 pieces for each hour after that. So, for a two-hour cocktail party, 10 pieces per person. In most cases, you can stop serving food after about three hours. But, if the party is going on for longer, after a break serve some tiny toasted sandwiches, little sausages in tiny bread rolls, or mini pizzas.

If you are trying to keep your drinks party within a time frame, it's a good idea to change from savoury to sweet about two-thirds of the way through – serve some sweet tartlets or strawberry-dipped chocolates, and perhaps even offer coffee.

As a rule of thumb, the more people at a party the less they eat per head. (And in most cases, the more people at a party, the more they drink per head.)

Even professional caterers stock some standbys in case of an emergency. So have some good-quality cheese and biscuits, or a fruit platter, on hand just in case.

what to choose

Keep it simple. Restrict the variety and just do a few things brilliantly. There's nothing wrong with the classics (they *are* classics because people love them), but it's nice to have a few unusual offerings.

Choose the freshest, best-quality ingredients – that doesn't mean it has to be oysters, but it does mean the best quality of whatever you choose. Think seasonal – vine-ripened baby tomatoes in summer, asparagus spears in spring, petite pumpkin pies in winter. This also ensures good quality at more reasonable prices.

When choosing your menu, you need to take into account (within reason) at least some of your friends' dietary requirements – for example, those who don't eat meat or are allergic nuts.

Aim for a balance of tastes and textures: include hot and cold, spicy and crisp, rich and creamy. Serve cold foods first, followed by hot food.

presentation

Party food should taste good *and* look good. Arrange your delicious delicacies so that guests simply can't resist. Serve samosas on a silver platter, wontons in a bamboo steamer, sandwiches in a napkin-lined basket, or prawn satays on glossy banana leaves. Serve oysters and scallops on the shell or in spoons, or noodle salad in mini take-away noodle boxes. But perhaps don't do all those at once! Choose a theme, a style, and stay with it.

preparation

Many of the recipes included in this book can be prepared ahead of time. That might be a few days ahead or, in some cases, several weeks ahead and then frozen. Look for the symbol ⊙, which flags do-ahead tips; and ❄ for information on freezing.

If you don't have any help, or you don't want to be stuck in the kitchen for most of your party, choose food that can be prepared ahead and doesn't need too much last-minute attention. Or choose only one or two items at the most.

When preparing food, take extra care to keep it as hygienic as possible – covered, and stored at the correct temperature.

refrigerating food

- Allow food to cool, then place in fridge. Make sure to keep refrigerated food well covered.

freezing food

- Allow to cool before freezing.
- Arrange in single layers, with non-stick freezer paper between layers
- Pastry items, especially puff pastry, should be cooked from frozen.
- If defrosting meat, defrost it in the fridge.

reheating food

For most items, unless stated otherwise, preheat the oven to about 150–180°C. If the food might dry out, cover with aluminium foil. Some items may need just a short time in the oven after reheating, to crisp them.

10 top party tips

- Keep it simple. Don't try to do too much – limit the variety of food and drink, but do it really well.
- Have plenty of sparkling clean glasses (at least two per person).
- Don't stint on the quality of wine or other alcohol (well – at least don't choose the cheapest there is!).
- Have plenty of non-alcoholic drinks, sparkling mineral water and iced water.
- Have someone in charge of drinks.
- Enlist someone to help serving food.
- If your party is near a mealtime, serve food early.
- Have heaps of table napkins and bowls to take discarded cocktail sticks, olive pips and the like.
- Remember – practice makes perfect: the more parties you have the better you will be at it.
- Enjoy!

small bites

Small and delicate, tiny and tasty or petite with punch – whichever style of finger food you choose, it should be finger-sized and bite-sized – just small enough to fit between two elegantly poised fingers and small enough to be consumed in one or two mouthfuls.

Choose several recipes – but not too many, unless you have an army of helpers. Aim for balance in both the style and the flavours. Perhaps start with something cold, and when more guests have arrived move onto some hot dishes. Serve something rich or special – it is a party after all – but also something for those inevitably watching their health or their waistline.

Passing the food around makes sure everyone has some, but if you don't have help, you can also position platters of finger food strategically so that guests can choose something and continue to mingle. Make a little extra effort on the presentation, offer stacks of napkins, and your party is well under way. If there are cocktail sticks, or satay skewers, or similar, provide plenty of places for guests to put discarded ones.

< angels on horseback (page 10)

angels on horseback

3–4 rashers rindless bacon
30 oysters, freshly shucked and drained
freshly ground black pepper
30 cocktail sticks

Preheat oven to 220°C.

Cut bacon into strips about 2 cm wide. Place each oyster on a strip of bacon, season lightly with freshly ground pepper, roll up and fasten with a cocktail stick.

Arrange on a non-stick baking tray, place in preheated oven and bake for 5–6 minutes, until bacon is sizzling and cooked. (You can cook them under a hot grill if you prefer.) Be careful not to overcook, or the oysters will be tough. Serve hot.

makes 30

variation
devils on horseback – substitute 30 soft pitted prunes, for the oysters.

Assemble up to 8 hours ahead. (Prunes version – assemble up to 3 days ahead; cook just before serving)

asparagus & beef with cream

24 fresh asparagus spears (same size, medium thickness)
12 thin slices rare roast beef
2 tablespoons sour cream
2 tablespoons grain mustard

Trim asparagus spears to about 7 cm long and discard ends. Boil or steam asparagus until barely cooked (it should still be quite crisp), then dip into iced water to refresh. Drain well and leave to cool.

Trim any visible fat from the beef and cut the slices in half. Mix the sour cream with the grain mustard.

Spread a layer of mustard cream on each slice of beef, place an asparagus spear near one edge, with the tip extending beyond the meat, and roll up. Arrange on a platter, and serve.

makes 24

Assemble up to 1 day ahead; store covered in fridge.

asparagus puffs

20 asparagus spears
2½ sheets ready-rolled puff pastry
½ cup grated parmesan cheese
1 egg beaten
2 tablespoons caraway seeds

Trim asparagus spears to about 10 cm long and discard ends. Boil or steam asparagus for a few minutes until just barely cooked. Dip into iced water to refresh, then drain.

Preheat oven to 200°C. Lightly oil a non-stick baking tray.

Cut pastry into 6-cm squares. Scatter some parmesan cheese over a pastry square, then lay an asparagus spear across one corner at an angle. Roll up pastry, leaving asparagus tip extending at one end, and press lightly to seal. Brush pastry with beaten egg and lay seam-side down on prepared tray. Scatter with some caraway seeds. Place in preheated oven and bake for 15–20 minutes, until pastry is puffed and golden. Serve warm.

makes 20

Make, or prepare to cooking stage, up to 1 day ahead; if cooked, reheat in preheated 180°C oven for 10–12 minutes.

baby baked potatoes

20 chat (or baby new) potatoes

3 tablespoons olive oil

coarsely ground sea salt

freshly ground black pepper

½ cup sour cream

25 g sharp blue cheese, crumbled

2–3 tablespoons chopped chives

Preheat oven to 180°C. Lightly oil a non-stick baking dish or tray.

Put potatoes, oil and salt and pepper in a bowl and toss to coat. Spread potatoes on prepared tray. Place in preheated oven and bake for 40–45 minutes until soft.

Meanwhile, mix sour cream and blue cheese until combined.

Remove potatoes from oven and allow to cool a little. With a sharp knife cut a cross in the top of each potato and use your fingers to push the potato open. Arrange potatoes on a serving platter, top each with a spoonful of the cream and sprinkle with chives. Serve warm or at room temperature.

makes 20

Cream and cheese – mix up to 4 days ahead. Potatoes – bake 2–3 hours ahead.

bacon & egg toast cups

12 slices sliced bread
(white or wholemeal)

2 eggs, lightly beaten

2 tablespoons cream

salt and freshly ground black
pepper

1 tablespoon butter

2 rashers bacon, chopped and
then fried until crisp

2 tablespoons finely chopped
chives

Preheat oven to 180°C. Lightly oil a 12-hole non-stick mini-muffin pan.

Use a rolling pin to flatten the bread. Use a cookie cutter to cut 6-cm
rounds of bread, then press these into prepared muffin pan. Place in
preheated oven and bake for 9–10 minutes, or until crisp.

Mix eggs with cream and season with salt and pepper. Melt butter in a
small non-stick saucepan over low heat, then add egg mix and stir until
scrambled.

Fill the cups with warm scrambled egg, top with some crumbled bacon,
sprinkle with a few chives and serve warm.

makes 12

Toast cups – make up to 2 weeks ahead; store in airtight container.
Fill just before serving.

brie, fig & walnut pizzette

180 g brie, cut into slices
¾ cup preserved figs, sliced
¼ cup chopped fresh walnuts
1 teaspoon fresh rosemary leaves
freshly ground black pepper

PIZZA DOUGH
2 cups plain flour
1 × 8-g sachet dry yeast
1 teaspoon caster sugar
½ teaspoon salt
2 tablespoons olive oil
¾ cup warm water

To make dough, combine all dry ingredients in large mixing bowl. Add oil and water and, using your hands, mix to a soft dough.

Knead on a lightly floured surface for a few minutes until soft and pliable. Return dough to the bowl, cover with plastic wrap and leave in a warm place for 30 minutes.

Meanwhile, preheat oven to 200°C. Lightly oil 1 or 2 non-stick baking trays.

When dough has doubled in size, punch it once to remove air bubbles. Remove from bowl and knead gently for 1 minute. Roll the dough out fairly thinly and cut small rounds (about 5 cm).

Spread preserved figs over the pizzette bases. Lay brie slices on top and scatter with the walnuts, rosemary and a twist of freshly ground black

>

pepper. Place in preheated oven and bake for 15 minutes or until base is crisp and puffed and cheese is bubbling.

Serve immediately.

makes about 20

Pizzette are best cooked just before serving, as brie does not reheat well.

Can freeze pizza dough (uncooked) for up to 2 months; defrost before baking.

bruschetta

1 loaf good-quality sourdough
or ciabatta bread
3–4 cloves garlic, halved
extra-virgin olive oil

Cut bread into slices about 1.5 cm thick and cut into halves or quarters to make bite-sized bases. Lightly toast or grill bread on both sides. Rub with cut garlic, then brush with a little olive oil.

Top with one of the following, just before serving (or lay out bases with bowls of ingredients for guests to create their own).

suggested toppings:

- black-olive tapenade (page 210), cherry bocconcini, fresh basil
- blue cheese, asparagus, lemon juice, flat-leaf parsley
- caramelised onions, black olives, fresh oregano
- grilled eggplant, fresh mozzarella, fresh basil
- crème fraîche, marinated baby mushrooms, fresh mint
- crushed cannellini beans, black olives
- fresh goat's curd, slow-roasted cherry tomatoes, fresh thyme
- goat's cheese, grilled red capsicum, crispy prosciutto
- jamon, asparagus, extra-virgin olive oil

>

- prosciutto, marinated artichokes, fresh mint
- smoked salmon, mustard mayo, fresh dill
- taleggio, wilted spinach, toasted walnuts
- vine-ripened tomatoes, extra garlic, slivered black olives, flat-leaf parsley
- wild rocket, gorgonzola cheese, slivers of fresh pear

makes about 30

Assemble close to serving time.

buckwheat blini with crème fraîche & salmon

½ cup plain flour

pinch salt

½ teaspoon baking powder

½ teaspoon bicarbonate soda

1 tablespoon caster sugar

½ cup buckwheat flour

1 egg, beaten

1½ cups buttermilk

30 g butter, melted

vegetable oil for frying

TOPPING

¾ cup crème fraîche

75 g smoked salmon slices

fresh dill, to serve

Sift dry ingredients together into a large bowl.

In a small bowl, combine egg, buttermilk and melted butter, and mix well. Add this mixture to the dry ingredients and stir until just combined (don't overmix). Leave batter to rest for 30 minutes.

Heat a heavy-based frying pan over medium heat and lightly oil. Use a spoon to pour in batter to make blini about 3–4 cm in diameter. Cook until bubbles appear on the surface, then turn and cook until lightly golden on the other side (about 1 minute).

When blini have cooled, top with a small scoop of crème fraîche, a sliver of smoked salmon and a little dill. Serve at room temperature.

makes about 30

Blini – make up to 1 day ahead; assemble everything up to 3 hours before serving.

cheesy rounds

75 g plain flour
100 g butter, at room temperature
75 g tasty cheese, finely grated
3 tablespoons sesame seeds
pinch cayenne pepper

Preheat oven to 190°C. Line a baking tray with non-stick baking paper.

Place all ingredients in a bowl and blend with an electric mixer or a spoon to form a dough. Roll the dough into small balls and place on prepared tray. Flatten lightly using the palm of your hand.

Place in preheated oven and bake for 10–15 minutes until crisp and pale gold. Cool on a cooling rack.

makes 30

Make up to 3 days ahead; store in airtight container.

cherry peppers with herbed goat's cheese

20 sweet or hot cherry peppers

4 cups white wine vinegar

1 cup soft goat's cheese

2 tablespoons very finely chopped fresh herbs
(e.g. oregano or mint)

Cut the tops off the cherry peppers and remove seeds and pith. Rinse peppers, then place in a non-metallic container and cover with vinegar. Place a plate on top to keep peppers submerged, and refrigerate overnight.

Mix goat's cheese and herbs, and also refrigerate overnight.

When ready to assemble, drain the peppers. Fill with cheese mix, arrange on a platter, and serve.

makes 20

Assemble up to 5 days ahead; store covered in fridge.

cherry tomatoes with pesto

20 cherry tomatoes

1 cup pesto (page 216)

Cut the tops off the tomatoes, then scoop out the inside using a small sugar spoon or melon baller. Turn shells upside to drain for 10 minutes.

Spoon pesto into tomatoes, arrange on a platter and chill for about an hour before serving.

makes 20

Assemble up to 3 hours ahead; keep refrigerated.

chicken batons with mayo

2 egg whites, well beaten

2 tablespoons plain flour

2 cups corn flakes, finely crushed

1 cup dry breadcrumbs

salt and freshly ground black
pepper

500 g chicken breast fillet
(skinless), sliced into strips
2 cm wide

vegetable oil for baking tray

classic mayo (page 211),
for dipping

Preheat oven to 180°C. Lightly oil a large non-stick baking tray.

Put egg whites and flour in separate bowls. Mix cornflakes, breadcrumbs,
salt and pepper in another bowl. Dip the chicken strips into egg white, then
into flour, then into the cornflake-crumb mix, pressing to coat the chicken.

Place chicken on prepared baking tray, place in preheated oven and bake
for about 20 minutes, turning once.

Serve hot or warm with lemon mayo.

makes 12–15

Make 1 day ahead (cooked or uncooked); store covered in fridge;
reheat in preheated 180°C oven for about 10 minutes.

chicken bites with plum sauce

600 g lean chicken mince

1½ cups fresh soft breadcrumbs

2 tablespoons finely chopped
fresh coriander

1 tablespoon grated fresh ginger

6 spring onions (white parts only),
thinly sliced

2 small eggs, lightly beaten

plum sauce, to serve

Put chicken, breadcrumbs, coriander, ginger, onions and eggs in a blender
or food processor and pulse until combined. Using wet hands, shape
mixture into about 20 small balls. Place on lightly oiled non-stick oven tray
and refrigerate for 10 minutes.

Preheat oven to 200° C.

Place tray of chicken bites in preheated oven and bake for 20–25 minutes,
turning once, until golden-brown. Serve hot or warm, with plum sauce.

makes 20

Make up to 2 days ahead; reheat, covered with foil, in preheated
180°C oven for 10–15 minutes.

chicken, pistachio & mayo sandwiches

3 chicken breast fillets (skinless)

salt and freshly ground pepper

1 sprig of fresh rosemary

1 cup good-quality mayonnaise (page 211)

2 tablespoons sour cream

3 tablespoons chopped pistachios

2 tablespoon chopped chives

butter or margarine, at room temperature

12 slices white or light wholemeal bread, crusts removed

In a saucepan or frying pan, heat enough water to cover chicken fillets. Add salt, pepper and rosemary and, when water is bubbling, add the chicken. Cover and simmer over very low heat for 5–6 minutes, then leave in water for 10 minutes to cool. Remove and drain, set aside for 10 minutes, then shred.

Place chicken, mayonnaise, sour cream, pistachios and chives in a bowl and mix well. Lightly butter bread to edges. Spread chicken mixture over half of the bread slices, then top with remaining slices. Cut into 3 to make ribbon sandwiches (an electric knife does this best).

Cover with plastic wrap until ready to serve. (See cocktail sandwiches, page 41, for other sandwich ideas.)

makes 36

Make up to 3 hours ahead; keep well covered.

chickpea & fetta patties
with tahini sauce

1 × 400-g can chickpeas, rinsed and drained

½ teaspoon ground coriander

1 egg

2 tablespoons plain flour

2 spring onions, thinly sliced

2 tablespoons chopped fresh coriander

200 g fetta cheese, crumbled

salt and freshly ground black pepper

olive oil, for frying

TAHINI SAUCE

½ cup Greek-style yoghurt

2 tablespoons tahini (see page 249)

1 tablespoon freshly squeezed lemon juice

generous pinch of salt

To make the tahini sauce, mix all ingredients until blended and refrigerate until needed.

Place the chickpeas, ground coriander, egg, flour and spring onions in a blender or food processor and blend until almost smooth.

Spoon chickpea mixture into a bowl, add fresh coriander and fetta, and stir to combine. Check seasoning and add salt and pepper if needed. Form mixture into small balls, then flatten into patties.

Heat oil in a non-stick frying pan over medium heat and shallow-fry patties in batches for 5–6 minutes, or until brown all over. Drain on crumpled kitchen paper.

Serve hot or at room temperature, with tahini sauce for dipping.

makes about 30

Make up to 3 days ahead; reheat, covered with foil. in preheated 180°C oven for 10–15 minutes.

chipolatas with honey & mustard

1 tablespoon vegetable oil

24 chipolata sausages

2 tablespoons honey

2 tablespoons Dijon mustard

extra Dijon mustard, to serve

Preheat oven to 180°C.

Pour oil into baking tray and place in oven for 3–4 minutes. When oil is hot, add chipolatas, shake pan to coat them with oil and return to oven. Roast for 25 minutes until golden-brown.

Meanwhile, mix honey and mustard until well blended.

Remove chipolatas from oven, drain on kitchen paper, then put them into a clean baking dish. Pour over honey–mustard mix and shake to coat sausages. Put dish back in oven for 5–6 minutes to heat.

Serve chipolatas hot or warm, with cocktail sticks and extra Dijon mustard on the side. (To make mini 'hot dogs': buy long dinner rolls and fill with a rocket leaf, a chipolata and a little extra mustard.)

makes 24

Chipolatas – roast 1 day ahead; drain, and store covered in fridge. To serve, coat with honey–mustard mix and heat in oven for 15 minutes.

chorizo & red wine tapas

600 g cured (ready-to-eat) chorizo sausages

2 cups light red wine (a Spanish Rioja or a pinot noir)

½ teaspoon whole black peppercorns

generous sprig of fresh rosemary

olive oil for cooking

1 tablespoon finely chopped flat-leaf parsley

Prick sausages all over. Place in a bowl, pour wine over, add peppercorns and rosemary, then cover and marinate for 24 hours. Drain.

Brush a large non-stick frying pan with oil, or lightly oil a barbecue grill. Cook sausage over a medium heat for 6–8 minutes until well cooked and crispy. Slice into thick chunks, cutting on the angle. Pierce with cocktail sticks, arrange on a platter, scatter with fresh parsley and serve immediately.

makes about 30

Chorizos – can marinate for up to 2 days.

chorizo turnovers

120 g cured (ready-to-eat) chorizo sausage, finely chopped
½ cup grated mild tasty cheese
3 sheets ready-rolled puff pastry
1 egg, lightly beaten, to glaze

Preheat oven to 200°C. Line a baking tray with non-stick baking paper.

Mix the chorizo and cheese in a small bowl.

Cut 8-cm circles from the pastry. Place a teaspoon of the chorizo and cheese on a pastry circle, moisten edges of pastry with water, fold over to make a pastie shape and press to seal. Repeat with remaining mixture.

Place turnovers on prepared tray, brush with beaten egg to glaze. Bake in preheated oven for 12–15 minutes, until puffed and golden. Transfer to a cooling rack for 5 minutes before serving.

Serve warm.

makes about 15

Make up to 2 days ahead; refrigerate. Reheat in preheated 180°C oven for about 10 minutes.

Can freeze (uncooked) for up to 2 months; cook from frozen, allowing 25–30 minutes.

cocktail sandwiches

Making the perfect cocktail sandwich – all you need to know

- Buy ready-sliced bread – white, wholemeal or grain.
- If using butter it should be at room temperature.
- Spread butter or margarine right to the edges of the bread.
- Use good-quality ingredients and make sure they are fresh.
- Make up your sandwiches and then cut off crusts (for more delicate sandwiches).
- Use an electric knife or sharp serrated knife for best cutting.
- Cut sandwiches into triangles to make points; into strips to make fingers or ribbons; or into shapes such as circles or hearts (use a sharp biscuit or cookie cutter to do this).
- Be generous with the filling, but don't use too many different ingredients.
- Serve a maximum of three varieties of filling on the one platter.
- Keep sandwiches covered with a damp tea-towel or plastic wrap until as close to serving time as possible.

a few suggested fillings:

- blue cheese with celery & toasted pecans
- crab meat, avocado & chives
- goat's cheese with roasted vegetables
- rare roast beef with horseradish & watercress

>

- ripe brie with sliced strawberries
- shaved leg ham & French mustard
- smoked salmon, cream cheese & capers
- tuna, mayo & slivered black olives
- turkey, cranberry & mustard cress

See also page 33 for chicken, pistachio & mayo sandwiches.

coconut chicken strips with saffron aioli

¼ cup plain flour

2 eggs, lightly beaten

1½ cups shredded coconut

1 cup soft fresh breadcrumbs

500 g chicken breast fillets (skinless), cut into long strips about 2 cm wide

sunflower or vegetable oil for deep-frying

SAFFRON AIOLI

generous pinch of saffron threads

1 tablespoon boiling water

1 cup good-quality mayonnaise (page 211)

1 clove garlic, crushed

1 tablespoon freshly squeezed lemon juice

To make saffron aioli, mix saffron threads with boiling water, stir well and then leave for 10 minutes. Whisk saffron liquid into the mayonnaise, then stir through the garlic and lemon juice. Cover, and refrigerate for at least 15 minutes before using.

Put flour and eggs into separate bowls. Mix coconut and breadcrumbs in another bowl. Dip chicken pieces into flour and shake off any excess. Now dip pieces into egg, then into the coconut and breadcrumbs. Place on a baking dish or flat tray, cover, and refrigerate for 15 minutes.

>

Heat oil for deep-frying. (To test if oil is hot enough, drop in a small cube of bread. If it sizzles and browns in about 10 seconds the oil is ready). Deep-fry chicken strips in batches until golden, and drain on crumpled kitchen paper.

Serve immediately, with saffron aioli alongside for dipping.

makes 12–14

Make up to 2 days ahead; reheat, covered with foil, in preheated 180°C oven for about 10 minutes.

coconut-crusted prawns
with lemon-zest yoghurt

1 kg medium-sized green (raw) prawns, peeled and deveined but tails left intact

1 cup rice flour

3 eggs, lightly beaten

3 cups shredded coconut

vegetable or peanut oil for deep-frying

LEMON-ZEST YOGHURT

1 cup Greek-style yoghurt

1 tablespoon freshly squeezed lemon juice

2 teaspoons grated lemon zest

To make the lemon-zest yoghurt, mix all ingredients in a small bowl, cover, and refrigerate for at least 30 minutes or until needed.

Rinse prawns quickly and pat dry.

Place flour, eggs and coconut in separate bowls. Holding prawns by the tail, dip each one into flour (dust off excess) and then dip into the egg and lastly the coconut, pressing lightly to ensure prawns are coated. Place on a plate and refrigerate if not cooking immediately.

Heat enough oil for deep-frying in a heavy-based saucepan over medium heat until hot. To test, drop a small cube of bread into oil – it should sizzle and brown in about 10 seconds. Add several prawns and cook for 1–2 minutes until golden-brown. Remove with a slotted spoon, drain on crumpled kitchen paper and keep warm.

>

Repeat with remaining prawns (make sure oil is hot enough before adding each batch).

Arrange prawns on serving platter and serve hot with the lemon-zest yoghurt in a bowl or bowls.

makes about 15

Prawns – coat up to 2 hours ahead; refrigerate. Cook just before serving.

crepes rolled
with salmon & capers

6 eggs

¼ cup milk

salt and freshly ground black pepper

vegetable oil

250 g light cream cheese

juice and zest of 1 lemon

250 g smoked salmon slices

2 tablespoons small capers, drained

Lightly whisk together eggs, milk, salt and plenty of freshly ground pepper.

Heat a non-stick omelette pan or 20-cm non-stick frying pan over medium heat and brush with a just enough oil to coat the pan. When oil is hot, pour in ¼ cup of egg mixture and swirl pan so it covers the base. Cook for 1–2 minutes (you don't need to turn the crepe, as it will cook through). Slide onto a chopping board and set aside to cool. Repeat process with remaining egg mixture.

Beat cream cheese, lemon juice and zest until well mixed. Spread a little onto each crepe, then top with smoked salmon slices and scatter over some capers. Roll up crepes firmly, cover and refrigerate for 1–2 hours. Use a very sharp knife to trim ends, then slice rolls into 2.5–3cm portions. Stand rolls on their side and serve.

makes about 40

Make up to 1 day ahead; keep covered in fridge. It's best to cut the crepes into serving portions on the day.

crisp baby cutlets
with pomegranate molasses

¾ cup plain flour

2 eggs, lightly beaten

2 cups panko breadcrumbs
(see page 249)

¾ cup sesame seeds

12 baby lamb cutlets

vegetable oil for frying

1 cup thick pomegranate
molasses (see page 249),
to serve

Put flour and eggs in separate bowls. Combine breadcrumbs and sesame seeds in another bowl.

Pat cutlets dry. Dip them into flour and dust off any excess, dip first into the beaten egg and then into the breadcrumbs and sesame seeds, pressing lightly to coat.

Heat oil in a non-stick frying pan over medium heat. When hot, fry cutlets for about 5 minutes on each side, or until browned and cooked through. Drain on kitchen paper.

Arrange on a serving platter, add a small spoonful of pomegranate molasses on top of each cutlet. Cutlets can be served hot or warm.

makes 12

Coat cutlets up to 2 days ahead (then refrigerate), but cook close to serving time.

crispy noodle
tartlets with chicken salad

100 g kataifi pastry

olive or vegetable oil

CHICKEN SALAD

250 g skinless chicken breast

1 tablespoon soy sauce

2 tablespoons freshly squeezed lime juice

1 tablespoon finely chopped fresh coriander

1 tablespoon finely chopped fresh mint

1 tablespoon finely sliced spring onion

2 tablespoons chopped dry-roasted peanuts

salt and freshly ground pepper, to taste

chilli sauce

Preheat oven to 180°C. Lightly oil two 12-hole non-stick mini-muffin trays.

Pull kataifi pastry apart and shape into 20 balls. Push pastry balls into muffin holes, pressing to form tart shapes. Spray or brush with oil, place tray in preheated oven and bake for 5 minutes until golden. Cool on a rack.

To make chicken salad, in a saucepan or frying pan heat enough water to cover chicken fillet. Add soy sauce and, when water is bubbling, the chicken breast, cover, then simmer over low heat for 5–6 minutes. Leave chicken in water for 10 minutes to cool, then remove from water, drain and pat dry. Leave for about 10 minutes (this will make it easier to cut), then finely shred or dice.

>

Place chicken in a bowl with the other salad ingredients, except the chilli sauce, and mix well.

Pile chicken salad into noodle cases, add a dollop of chilli sauce and serve immediately.

makes about 20

Pastry cases – make up to 3 days ahead; store in airtight container. Tartlets – assemble up to 15 minutes before serving. Salad – make 1 day ahead; refrigerate.

crudités with dips

Crudités, the clever French way of eating crisp, fresh vegetables with a garlicky aioli or other dip, is a great idea for a party, either as finger food or as part of a platter on a buffet table.

Limit the variety of vegetables, depending on the number of guests, to perhaps four or five types. Make sure they are as fresh as can be, crisp, very well prepared (neatly sliced and trimmed) and cut into bite-sized pieces. Baby vegetables (e.g. carrots, sweetcorn) are ideal.

Arrange the vegetables in neat bundles or piles with contrasting colours and keep refrigerated and crisp until it's time to serve them.

Here are a few suggestions:

- asparagus (blanched if you prefer)
- baby green beans
- baby sweetcorn
- cauliflower, broken into florets
- celery, cut into 5 cm-long sticks
- button mushrooms
- cherry tomatoes
- cucumber, cut into 5 cm-long sticks
- dutch carrots
- red and yellow capsicums, cut into thin strips

>

- snow peas (blanched if you prefer)
- whole baby radishes

To serve on the side, try classic mayonnaise (page 211) or a variation such as wasabi mayo, or a home-made hummus (page 213).

cucumber, rare beef & dijonnaise

5 Lebanese cucumbers
5 small slices rare roast beef
3 tablespoons Dijonnaise (see page 248)
1 tablespoon chopped fresh chives

Peel cucumbers, trim ends and cut into slices about 2.5 cm thick. Scoop out seeds and place on a tray to drain for 10 minutes.

Cut beef into small strips about 2 cm × 5 cm. Curl beef to create a rose shape and push into the cucumber round. Top with a little Dijonnaise and arrange on serving platter. Sprinkle a few chives over each cucumber round.

makes 20

Make up to 3 hours ahead; keep refrigerated.

curried potato & pea triangles

500 g potatoes, peeled and diced

½ teaspoon ground turmeric

1 onion, finely chopped

1 cup shelled peas, fresh or frozen

½ teaspoon ground cardamom

1 teaspoon cumin seeds

1 teaspoon curry powder

2 tablespoons freshly squeezed lime juice

salt

12 sheets spring-roll pastry

peanut or vegetable oil, for deep-frying

Put potatoes in a medium-sized saucepan, add turmeric and enough boiling water to cover, and cook for 5–6 minutes or until tender. Drain thoroughly.

Add onion, peas (defrost first, if using frozen), cardamom, cumin seeds, curry powder and lime juice to the potatoes, and season with salt to taste. Stir to combine.

Cut 1 pastry sheet into 3 strips. Put a small spoonful of filling on one end and fold pastry to form a triangle. Continue folding to make a neat triangular parcel. Moisten the final edge with water and press to fasten.

In a heavy-based saucepan, heat enough oil for deep-frying. When hot, add the prepared triangles a few at a time and fry until golden. Drain on

crumpled kitchen paper and keep warm while you cook the remainder.
Arrange triangles on a platter and serve hot.

makes about 36

Make up to 2 days ahead; refrigerate. Reheat in preheated 180°C oven
for about 10 minutes.

Can freeze (uncooked) for up to 2 months; cook from frozen.

devilled eggs

10 small eggs, at room temperature

100 g soft goat's cheese

100 ml milk

4 spring onions, finely chopped

3 tablespoons finely chopped basil leaves

½ teaspoon ground cayenne

salt and freshly ground black pepper

2 tablespoons finely chopped chives, to serve

Place eggs in one layer in a saucepan, cover with cold water, bring to the boil, reduce heat and simmer for 3 minutes. Turn off heat, cover, and leave for 10 minutes. Drain water, rinse eggs with cold water and crack the shells. Leave until cool enough to handle, then peel off shells.

Use a sharp knife to cut the eggs in half lengthways. Scoop out the yolks, place in a bowl and mash with the goat's cheese, milk, spring onions, basil, cayenne, and salt and pepper to taste. Mix well. Put mixture into a piper and pipe into the whites (or use a teaspoon), piling mixture high. Arrange on a platter, scatter chives over the top, and serve.

makes 20

Eggs – boil up to 2 days ahead; refrigerate. Fill up to 8 hours ahead; cover with cling wrap and keep refrigerated.

dolmades with pistachios & lemon

250 g vine leaves in brine

¾ cup olive oil

2 onions, finely chopped

1 clove garlic, crushed

¾ cup short-grain rice, rinsed

3 spring onions, sliced

¼ teaspoon ground cinnamon

finely grated zest of 1 lemon

2 tablespoons finely chopped fresh dill

2 tablespoons finely chopped fresh mint

60 g unsalted, shelled pistachios, chopped

salt and freshly ground black pepper

1½ cups vegetable stock

lemon wedges, to serve

Soak vine leaves in warm water for at least 1 hour, then rinse and pat dry.

Heat ½ cup oil in a large frying pan over low heat. Add onions and garlic, and sauté for 4–5 minutes until softened but not brown. Add rice, spring onions, cinnamon, lemon zest, herbs, pistachios, salt and freshly ground pepper. Mix well.

Lay a vine leaf, vein-side up, on a dry work surface. Place a spoonful of filling near the base of the leaf. Roll it once, fold in sides and then roll towards the tip of the leaf. Don't use too much filling and don't roll it too tightly, or the dolmades will burst when the rice swells. Continue until you have used all the filling.

>

Line the base of a heavy-based flameproof casserole or saucepan with 5 or 6 unfilled vine leaves. Put in the dolmades, seam-side down, packing them snugly, pour remaining oil over and put a plate on top to keep them in place. Pour stock over and bring slowly to the boil, then reduce heat, cover, and simmer for 45 minutes. Remove plate, and take out dolmades using a slotted spoon.

Serve warm or at room temperature. If serving as finger food (without plates) squeeze some lemon juice over the dolmades before serving.

makes about 30, depending on size of vine leaves

Make up to 5 days ahead; refrigerate.

empanaditas

2 tablespoons olive oil

1 clove garlic, crushed

1 onion, finely chopped

2 teaspoons ground cumin

350 g chicken breast fillet, diced

1 teaspoon finely sliced fresh red chilli

50 g green olives, pitted and sliced

2 tablespoons sultanas

2 eggs, hardboiled and finely chopped

2 tablespoons chopped fresh coriander

salt and freshly ground black pepper

1–2 tablespoons cream

4 sheets ready-rolled puff pastry

1 egg, beaten

Heat oil in a large non-stick frying pan over medium heat. When it is hot add the garlic and onion, and stir-fry for 3–4 minutes until softened. Add cumin and chicken, and cook, stirring occasionally, until chicken is cooked and any liquid has evaporated. Leave to cool.

Preheat oven to 200°C. Lightly grease or oil a non-stick baking tray.

Add chilli, olives, sultanas, egg and coriander to the chicken and season with salt and freshly ground pepper. Add just enough cream to help bind the mixture together.

>

Cut pastry into 8-cm circles. Place about 1 teaspoon of the chicken mixture on a pastry circle, fold over to form a crescent shape and pinch edges together. Place empanaditas on prepared tray and brush with beaten egg. Bake in preheated oven for 25 minutes, or until puffed and golden.

Serve hot or warm.

makes 24

Make up to 3 days ahead; reheat in preheated 180°C oven for about 15 minutes.

Can freeze (uncooked) for up to 2 months ahead; bake from frozen in preheated oven for 30–35 minutes, until puffed and golden.

figs with goat's cheese & fennel

20 small ripe figs, halved lengthways
100 g soft goat's cheese
1 tablespoon balsamic vinegar
1 tablespoon fennel seeds

Preheat oven to 180°C. Line a baking tray with non-stick baking paper.

Place figs, cut side up, on the baking tray, put a little cheese on each one, brush with a little balsamic and then sprinkle with a few fennel seeds.

Place in preheated oven and bake for 7–8 minutes, until figs are warmed. Arrange on a serving platter and serve while still warm.

makes 20

Prepare up to 1 day ahead; refrigerate covered. Return to room temperature before baking.

fish brochettes
with lime dipping sauce

600 g firm white fish fillets, cut into strips 2 cm wide

20 bamboo skewers, soaked in water for 30 minutes

¾ cup plain flour

salt and freshly ground black pepper

sunflower or vegetable oil for shallow-frying

LIME DIPPING SAUCE

½ cup lime juice

2 tablespoons fish sauce

2 tablespoons caster sugar

1 small clove garlic, crushed

2 tablespoons toasted sesame seeds

1 tablespoon finely chopped fresh coriander

To make dipping sauce, whisk ingredients together, cover, and leave for at least 1 hour for flavours to develop.

Thread fish strips lengthways onto skewers. Season flour with salt and pepper, and spread on a dish. Dip skewers into flour and dust off any excess.

Heat oil in a large frying pan over medium–high heat. Cook skewers until golden on all sides, turning once or twice (they should only take 1–2 minutes on each side). Serve immediately, with dipping sauce on the side.

makes 20

Dipping sauce – make up to 2 days ahead (add coriander just before serving). Fish – thread skewers 1 day ahead; coat with flour and cook just before serving.

french croutons with goat's curd

24 slices (about 1.5 cm thick)
French bread stick (baguette)

about 4 tablespoons olive oil

2 cloves garlic, cut in half

2 small onions, quartered

2 teaspoons brown sugar

salt

150 g goat's curd or soft goat's
cheese

fresh thyme leaves, to serve

Preheat oven to 200°C.

Brush bread slices lightly on each side with some of the oil, place on baking tray and bake in preheated oven for 15 minutes or until crisp and golden. Rub a cut garlic clove over one side of each crouton.

Slice onions very thinly. Heat remaining oil in a non-stick frying pan over medium heat, add onions and cook, stirring occasionally, for about 10 minutes until transparent. Add sugar and a pinch of salt, and cook for a few more minutes until onions are caramelised. Allow to cool.

Arrange croutons on a serving platter, top each with a small scoop of goat's curd, a little caramelised onion and a scattering of thyme leaves, and serve.

makes 24

Croutons – bake up to 3 days ahead; store in airtight container. Onions – cook up to 3 days ahead, and refrigerate; return to room temperature before serving. Assemble croutons as close to serving time as possible.

fresh figs with gorgonzola & prosciutto

10 small ripe figs, halved lengthways
(or use 5 larger ones and cut into quarters)

100 g gorgonzola (or other sharp blue) cheese

10 slices prosciutto

20 cocktail sticks

Trim top and bottom of figs. Spread a little gorgonzola on the cut surfaces.

Cut prosciutto slices in half. Wrap a piece of prosciutto around each fig and secure with a cocktail stick.

Arrange figs on a platter and serve.

makes 20

Make up to 1 day ahead; refrigerate well covered, so prosciutto doesn't dry out. Return to room temperature before serving.

green mango & chicken salad boxes

1 small, green (unripe) mango, peeled and cut into thin strips

200 g smoked chicken, diced

1 fresh red chilli, deseeded and finely sliced

1 fresh green chilli, deseeded and finely sliced

1 spring onion, finely sliced

1 tablespoon finely chopped fresh coriander leaves

½ cup chopped, roasted unsalted cashew nuts

2 tablespoons good-quality mayonnaise (page 211)

1 tablespoon freshly squeezed lime juice

extra coriander leaves, for garnish

10 mini Asian noodle take-away boxes

Place all the ingredients (except the coriander garnish) in a bowl and mix gently until combined. If mixture is dry, add a little extra mayonnaise or lime juice.

Spoon mixture into noodle boxes, scatter a few coriander leaves over, and serve with bamboo chopsticks or small forks.

makes 10

Salad – make 1 day ahead; keep refrigerated. Boxes – fill up to 4 hours ahead; refrigerate until close to serving time.

haloumi skewers
with lemon wedges

250 g haloumi cheese

3 tablespoons olive oil

16 bamboo skewers, soaked in water for 30 minutes

1 tablespoon finely chopped flat-leaf parsley, for garnish

lemon wedges, to serve

Pat haloumi dry. Cut into 8 slices, then cut slices in half to make 16 pieces. Thread haloumi onto bamboo skewers.

Preheat oven grill or barbecue to high. Brush cheese with oil and then grill skewers on one side until golden and sizzling. Turn skewers, and grill other side.

Arrange on a serving platter, scatter with parsley and serve immediately with lemon wedges.

makes 16

Assemble up to 2 days ahead; refrigerate covered. Grill just before serving.

herb frittatas with wasabi cream

2 eggs

2 tablespoons cream

1 tablespoon finely chopped fresh coriander leaves

1 teaspoon finely grated lemon zest

salt and freshly ground black pepper

2 tablespoons crème fraîche

½ teaspoon wasabi paste

extra coriander leaves, to serve

Preheat oven to 150°C. Lightly grease a 12-hole, non-stick mini-muffin pan.

Put eggs, cream, coriander, lemon zest, salt and pepper in a bowl and whisk until combined. Pour into muffin pan and bake in preheated oven for 6–8 minutes or until just set. Allow to cool before removing from pan.

Mix crème fraîche with wasabi to make wasabi cream. Top frittatas with a little wasabi cream and a coriander leaf, and serve.

makes 12

Frittatas – make 1 day ahead; refrigerate. Top with wasabi cream up to 1 hour before serving.

Indian paneer patties

1 cup Greek-style yoghurt

1 cup paneer (see page 249)

1 spring onion, finely chopped

3 tablespoons grated fresh ginger

3 tablespoons finely sliced fresh green chilli

1 tablespoon chopped fresh coriander leaves

$\frac{1}{2}$ teaspoon salt

$\frac{3}{4}$ cup chickpea flour (besan – see page 248)

sunflower or vegetable oil for deep-frying

First drain the yoghurt: line a colander or sieve with muslin, add yoghurt, tie cloth and allow to drain for at least half an hour. (You can leave the yoghurt to drain in the fridge overnight if you prefer.)

Put drained yoghurt and paneer in a bowl with onion, ginger, chilli, coriander and salt, and mix well. Shape mixture into small patties and dip into chickpea flour to coat. Place in fridge for 10–15 minutes.

Heat oil in a heavy-based saucepan or wok over high heat, then add patties a few at a time and fry until golden. Drain on kitchen paper and serve immediately.

makes 24

Prepare up to 2 days ahead; refrigerate. Cook just before serving.

keftedes with mint yoghurt

1 kg lean beef mince
½ cup fresh breadcrumbs
½ onion, finely chopped
1 clove garlic, crushed
1 tablespoon dried oregano
½ cup crumbled fetta cheese
1 egg, beaten
freshly ground black pepper
olive oil for shallow frying

1 cup Greek-style yoghurt
2 tablespoons finely chopped fresh mint leaves
1 tablespoon freshly squeezed lemon juice
a pinch of salt

To make mint yoghurt, mix all ingredients well, cover, and refrigerate for at least 30 minutes before serving.

To make keftedes, combine all the ingredients in a large bowl and mix well to combine. Cover mixture and refrigerate for half an hour.

Using wet hands, shape mixture into small balls. Heat about 2 cm of oil in a non-stick frying pan over medium heat. When it is hot, cook meatballs in batches until golden-brown and crisp all over (5–7 minutes, depending on size). Drain on kitchen paper.

>

Serve the keftedes hot or at room temperature, with mint yoghurt in small bowls for dipping.

makes 20–30

Keftedes – make up to 3 days ahead. Reheat, covered with foil, in preheated 180°C oven for about 15 minutes. Mint yoghurt – make up to 2 days ahead.

lamb tikka kebabs
with fresh coriander chutney

2 tablespoons tikka paste
(see page 250)

1 cup Greek-style yoghurt

12 lamb fillets, cut lengthways
into 2–3 strips (depending on
thickness)

bamboo skewers, soaked in water
for 30 minutes

olive oil for cooking

FRESH CORIANDER CHUTNEY

2 cups fresh coriander leaves
(loosely packed)

1 clove garlic, crushed

1 fresh green chilli, deseeded
and chopped

¼ cup desiccated coconut

2 tablespoons freshly squeezed
lemon juice

1–2 tablespoons water

salt

To make coriander chutney, put coriander, garlic, chilli, coconut, lemon
juice and water in a blender or food processor, and blend to a thick paste.
Test for seasoning, and add salt if required. Cover and refrigerate until
needed.

Meanwhile, blend tikka paste with yoghurt and coat the lamb fillets
with this mixture. Cover well, refrigerate, and marinate for 1–2 hours
or overnight.

When ready to cook, preheat oven grill or barbecue to high. Lightly oil
a non-stick baking tray.

>

Thread the lamb fillets onto the skewers. Grill or barbecue, turning once or twice, until cooked and tender. Serve hot, with coriander chutney on the side.

makes 24–30

Chutney – make up to 2 days ahead; refrigerate. Lamb – marinate up to 2 days ahead; grill just before serving.

lime & chilli grilled prawns

1 cup dry white wine

1 tablespoon grated fresh ginger

2 kaffir lime leaves, finely sliced

2 cloves garlic, crushed

2 long red chillies, deseeded and finely sliced

36 small to medium-sized green (raw) prawns, peeled and deveined but tails left intact

18 bamboo skewers, soaked in water for at least 30 minutes

¼ cup olive oil

lime wedges, to serve

Mix wine, ginger, lime leaves, garlic and chillies in a bowl. Add prawns, toss well, cover, and marinate in fridge for 1–2 hours.

Preheat oven grill or barbecue to high.

Thread 2 prawns on each skewer and brush lightly with oil. Grill or barbecue prawns, turning once or twice, until cooked through (depending on size of prawns and heat of grill, about 2 minutes).

Serve immediately, with lime wedges on the side.

makes 18

Marinade – prepare 2 days ahead. Prawns – marinate for up to 2–3 hours before grilling, but no longer as they will become tough.

lychees with prosciutto & mint

12 fresh (or drained, canned) lychees, peeled
6 slices prosciutto, cut in half lengthways
12 small fresh mint leaves
12 cocktail sticks

Use a sharp knife to make an incision in the lychees and remove the stones.

Wrap a piece of prosciutto around each lychee. Pierce a basil leaf with a cocktail stick, then thread a wrapped lychee onto each stick. Arrange on a platter to serve.

makes 12

⌄ Make up to 4 hours ahead; refrigerate.

mini sausage rolls
with plum sauce

½ cup fresh breadcrumbs

⅓ cup milk

250 g pork mince

250 g chicken mince

½ small onion, finely chopped

1 egg

1 tablespoon finely chopped
flat-leaf parsley

1 tablespoon finely chopped fresh
sage or thyme

freshly ground black pepper

2 sheets ready-rolled puff pastry

1 egg, lightly beaten, for glazing

plum sauce, to serve

Place breadcrumbs and milk in a bowl and leave for 5 minutes until milk is absorbed.

Place mince in a blender or food processor with the soaked breadcrumbs, onion and egg. Process until well combined. Stir fresh herbs and ground pepper through the mixture, cover, and refrigerate for 30 minutes.

Place 1 sheet of pastry on a lightly floured surface and cut lengthways into two. Spoon a quarter of the filling along the centre of each pastry strip, and brush one long edge with beaten egg. Fold pastry over and roll up to form a log. Repeat, to make 4 logs.

Preheat oven to 180°C. Line a large baking tray with non-stick baking paper.

>

Place logs on tray. Glaze top with beaten egg and sprinkle with sesame seeds. Cut each log into 10 (this makes quite small rolls). Place trays in preheated oven and bake for 20–25 minutes until pastry is puffed and golden-brown. Serve warm, with plum sauce.

makes 40

Make up to 2 days ahead; refrigerate. Reheat in preheated 200°C oven for about 15 minutes.

Can freeze (uncooked) for up to 4 weeks; cook from frozen.

moroccan spinach pies

2 tablespoons sultanas
or currants

1 tablespoon olive oil

2 cloves garlic, crushed

1 large bunch fresh spinach,
washed and chopped

5 anchovies in oil, drained
and chopped

1 teaspoon ras el hanout
(see page 249)

freshly ground black pepper

3 tablespoons pine nuts, toasted
and chopped

3 sheets ready-rolled puff pastry

1 egg, beaten, for glaze

Put the sultanas or currants in half a cup of warm water and leave to soak for 10 minutes. Drain and chop.

Heat oil in large non-stick saucepan or frying pan over medium heat. Add garlic and stir-fry for 1–2 minutes. Add spinach, cover, and cook for 3–4 minutes until spinach is wilted. (If there is any moisture left, drain spinach and return to pan.)

Add anchovies, ras el hanout and some black pepper to the pan and cook for 1 minute, stirring, until mixed. Remove from heat, add sultanas or currants, and pine nuts. Leave to cool.

Preheat oven to 200°C. Lightly oil a large non-stick baking tray.

>

From the pastry cut out circles 8 cm in diameter. Place a spoonful of filling in the middle of each pastry circle, moisten the edges with water, fold pastry over and press to close. Place on prepared tray, brush with beaten egg and bake in preheated oven for 15 minutes until golden.

Serve hot or warm.

makes 18–20

⊙ Make 1 day ahead and refrigerate. Reheat in preheated 180°C oven for about 10 minutes (if pastry is already browned, cover with aluminium foil).

❄ Can freeze (uncooked) for up to 4 weeks; cook from frozen, in preheated 200°C oven for 20–25 minutes or until puffed and golden.

mushroom & fontina toasts

225 g button or swiss brown mushrooms

2 tablespoons extra-virgin olive oil

pinch of salt

2 tablespoons sherry

12 slices French bread stick, about 2 cm thick

150 g fontina, gouda or taleggio cheese

Remove stalks from mushrooms and discard. Slice the mushroom caps thinly.

Heat oil in a frying over medium heat. When oil is hot, add mushrooms, salt and sherry, cover, and reduce heat. Cook until liquid is released from the mushrooms (about 10 minutes). Drain off liquid and set mushrooms aside.

Preheat grill to high.

Lightly toast bread slices, then top with mushrooms and a slice of fontina. Place under preheated grill until cheese starts to melt. Serve immediately.

makes 12

Mushrooms – cook 3 days ahead; refrigerate. Reheat in a saucepan, or return to room temperature, before putting on toast. Assemble and grill toasts just before serving.

mushrooms with
goat's cheese & bacon

36 medium-sized button
mushrooms

2 tablespoons olive oil

1 onion, finely chopped

250 g soft goat's cheese

pinch of grated nutmeg

freshly ground black pepper

1 bunch spinach, washed, cooked,
drained and finely chopped

200 g bacon rashers, cooked
and chopped

Wipe mushrooms and remove stalks.

Heat oil in small frying pan or saucepan and add the onion. Cook, stirring for 5–6 minutes until tender, then transfer to a bowl. When onion is cool, stir through goat's cheese, nutmeg and black pepper. Add spinach and bacon, and stir well.

Preheat oven to 180°C. Lightly oil a large baking tray.

Spoon filling into mushroom caps and place on prepared baking tray. Bake in preheated oven for 10–15 minutes. Arrange on a platter and serve warm.

makes 36

Filling – make up to 3 days ahead; refrigerate. Mushrooms – stuff up to 2 days ahead; refrigerate covered; bake just before serving.

olive & sage scones
with mascarpone

250 g potatoes, peeled and quartered

¼ cup chopped, pitted kalamata olives

½ cup milk

10 fresh sage leaves, chopped

2 cups self-raising flour

about ½ cup water

freshly ground black pepper

milk for glazing

30 g cold butter, chopped

mascarpone (see page 249), to serve

Preheat oven to 210°C. Lightly oil a non-stick baking tray.

Boil or steam potatoes until soft, then mash with the milk.

Sift flour into a large bowl and add some pepper. Add butter and rub in with fingertips. Add olives and sage leaves. Make a well in the centre, then add the mashed potato. Gradually add water, mixing with a flat-bladed knife, to make a dough. (You may not need all the water: the dough should not be too sticky.)

Put dough on a lightly floured board and knead lightly until smooth (don't over-handle). Press out to about 2-cm thickness, then use a pastry cutter to cut dough into 4-cm rounds.

>

Put scones on the prepared tray, brush tops with milk to glaze, and place in preheated oven. Bake for 12 15 minutes until golden.

Serve the scones warm or cold, cut in half, and spread with a little mascarpone.

makes 16

Best made on the day. But can be cooked up to 3 days ahead; reheat, covered with foil, in preheated !80°C oven for 6–7 minutes.
Can freeze (cooked) for up to 6 weeks. Reheat in preheated 180°C oven for about 10 minutes.

onion jam & olive pies

2 tablespoons butter

4 onions, quartered and finely sliced

freshly ground black pepper

200 g pitted kalamata olives, chopped

chopped leaves from 1 small bunch fresh thyme

about ⅔ cup chicken stock

2 sheets ready-rolled puff pastry

1 small egg, beaten

Heat butter in a non-stick saucepan or frying pan over medium heat. Add onions and sauté for 6–7 minutes until soft and transparent. Season with freshly ground pepper, then add the olives, thyme leaves and stock, and simmer until onions are caramelised and all the liquid absorbed. Leave to cool.

Preheat oven to 200°C. Lightly oil 2 × 12-hole mini-muffin pans, or 24 mini tart moulds.

Cut 24 circles of pastry with a 5-cm biscuit cutter and use these to line the pans or moulds. Cut another 24 circles for the lids.

Fill pastry cases with the onion mixture and top each with a lid. Glaze with beaten egg, then cut a slit in the centre of the lid with a sharp knife.

>

Place pies in preheated oven and bake for 15 minutes, until pastry is puffed
and golden. Serve warm.

makes 24

Cook 1 day ahead; reheat before serving.

Can freeze (uncooked) for up to 2 months; cook from frozen,
in preheated 200°C oven for 20 minutes.

oriental beef balls

1 cup fresh soft breadcrumbs

1 cup milk

1 kg good-quality beef mince

1 onion, finely chopped

2 tablespoons finely chopped
fresh coriander

1 tablespoon finely grated
fresh ginger

1 egg, lightly beaten

salt and freshly ground
black pepper

1 cup sesame seeds

sweet chilli sauce, to serve

Preheat oven to 180°C. Lightly oil a non-stick baking tray.

Soak the breadcrumbs in the milk for about 10 minutes. Drain, and squeeze
out milk (the bread will be pulpy). Place bread, mince, onion, coriander,
ginger and egg in a bowl and mix well. Season with salt and pepper.

Shape mixture into small, bite-sized balls and roll these lightly in sesame
seeds. Place on prepared tray and bake in preheated oven for about
20 minutes until golden on the outside and cooked through.

Serve hot, with sweet chilli sauce for dipping.

makes 24

Make up to 2 days ahead; store (cooked or uncooked) in fridge.
If cooked, reheat covered with foil in preheated 180°C oven for
about 10 minutes.

oyster shooters

12 oysters, freshly shucked and drained
250 ml ice-cold tomato juice
60 ml ice-cold vodka
1 tablespoon Worcestershire sauce
1 tablespoon freshly squeezed lime juice
freshly ground black pepper

Put the oysters into 12 shot glasses.

Shake tomato juice, vodka, Worcestershire sauce and lime juice until well mixed (use a cocktail shaker, if you have one), then pour over the oysters. Add a twist of black pepper and serve immediately.

makes 12

Tomato–vodka mix – make several days ahead; keep covered in fridge. Make shooters just before serving – the oysters should be as fresh as possible.

oysters with sake

2 spring onions, very finely sliced

2 tablespoons sunflower oil

1½ tablespoons mirin
(see page 249)

2 tablespoons sake

2 teaspoons finely grated
fresh ginger

2 teaspoons soy sauce

24 oysters, freshly shucked

Place all ingredients except oysters in a small bowl and stir until well mixed.

Place oysters on a bed of ice on a platter. Drizzle a teaspoonful of sauce over each oyster and serve immediately.

makes 24

Dressing – make up to 2 days ahead (add spring onions closer to serving time); return to room temperature before serving. Oysters – shuck as close to serving time as possible.

paprika parmesan pinwheels

2 sheets ready-rolled puff pastry
1½–2 cups grated parmesan cheese
2 teaspoons ground paprika
1 egg white, lightly beaten
2 tablespoons sesame seeds

Preheat oven to 200°C. Line a baking tray with non-stick baking paper.

Lay out one pastry sheet. Sprinkle with half the parmesan and 1 teaspoon of the paprika, then roll into a log. Brush with egg white and sprinkle with half the sesame seeds. Cut logs into 2-cm lengths and lay the pieces on the prepared tray. Repeat with remaining ingredients.

Place tray in preheated oven and bake for 10–12 minutes, until pinwheels are puffed and golden. Serve hot or warm.

makes 36

Prepare up to 2 days ahead; refrigerate uncooked. Bake just before serving.

Can freeze for up to 4 weeks; cook from frozen in preheated 200°C oven for 15–20 minutes.

parmesan chicken with lemon aioli

4 chicken breast fillets (skinless)

1½ cups fresh breadcrumbs

3 tablespoons finely grated
parmesan cheese

2 tablespoons finely chopped
flat-leaf parsley

salt and freshly ground pepper

2 eggs, beaten

50 g butter, melted

lemon aioli (page 215)

Lightly oil a non-stick baking tray.

Cut each chicken fillet into 4 or 5 strips. Mix together the breadcrumbs,
parmesan, parsley and some salt and pepper. Dip chicken in the eggs
and then in the breadcrumb mix. Place on prepared tray and refrigerate
for 30 minutes.

Preheat oven to 180°C.

Bake chicken pieces in preheated oven for 15–20 minutes until golden.
Serve hot with lemon aioli.

makes about 20

⌣ Chicken – cook up to 2 days ahead; reheat, covered with foil, in
preheated 180°C oven for 15 minutes. Aioli – make up to 3 days ahead;
refrigerate.

parmesan crisps

½ cup plain flour

3 tablespoons butter, at room temperature

1 egg yolk, lightly beaten

75 g freshly grated parmesan cheese

¼ teaspoon ground paprika

¼ teaspoon mustard powder

Put flour and butter in a bowl and rub together with your fingertips. Add egg, cheese and spices, and mix to form a dough. Shape dough into a log, wrap in cling wrap and refrigerate for 15 minutes.

Preheat oven to 220°C. Line a baking tray with non-stick baking paper.

Cut log into 1-cm rings and place on prepared tray. Press lightly with a fork. Place in preheated oven and bake for 10 minutes until crisp and golden (be careful not to let them burn).

Store in an airtight container.

makes 16

Make up to 3 days ahead; store in airtight container.

peking duck pancakes

1 Chinese barbecued duck
10 spring onions
30 bought Peking duck pancakes

hoisin sauce
2 Lebanese cucumbers,
cut into thin 5-cm sticks

Use a sharp knife to cut duck into small strips. Cover and keep warm.

Cut spring onions into 5-cm lengths, then make slits in one end of each onion piece, to make a 'brush'. Place pieces in iced water for 10 minutes, or until ready to use (this keeps them crisp).

Wrap pancakes in aluminium foil and warm in preheated oven, or heat in a microwave.

To assemble pancakes, use a spring onion 'brush' to brush hoisin sauce on a pancake, top with piece of duck, a piece of spring onion and a cucumber stick, and roll into a cylinder. Lay, seam-side down, on a serving platter.

Serve with a small bowl of extra hoisin sauce on the side.

makes 30

Spring onions and cucumber – prepare 1 day ahead; refrigerate. Assemble pancakes just before serving.

Persian potato kuku (omelette)

250 g shelled broad beans
(frozen are fine)

500 g potatoes, cooked and
mashed

5 eggs, beaten

½ teaspoon ground turmeric

½ teaspoon ground cardamom

¼ teaspoon ground cumin

4 spring onions, chopped

2 tablespoons finely chopped
fresh coriander

1 tablespoon chopped fresh dill

salt and freshly ground black
pepper

1–2 tablespoons olive oil

yoghurt or sour cream and
extra coriander leaves, to serve
(optional)

If using fresh broad beans, cook in boiling water for 3–4 minutes, then cool and pop off the skins. If using frozen beans, put them into a bowl, pour boiling water over and leave for a minute. Drain, and pop off the skins.

Put mashed potato in a large bowl, add eggs, turmeric, cardamom and cumin and mix well. Stir in the broad beans, spring onions, coriander and dill. Season to taste with salt and pepper.

Heat oil in a heavy-based, non-stick frying pan (about 25–30 cm diameter) over medium heat. When oil is hot, pour in potato mix, reduce heat to lowest temperature and leave to cook for 10–15 minutes.

Meanwhile, preheat oven grill to medium.

When eggs are set and base is golden-brown (check to make sure it is not burning), place pan under grill to lightly brown top. When cooked, transfer to a plate. Leave to cool a little, then cut into 3-cm cubes to serve warm or at room temperature. (If serving kuku at room temperature, top each piece with a small dollop of yoghurt or sour cream and a coriander leaf.)

makes about 30

Make 1 day ahead; keep covered in fridge. Return to room temperature and cut into squares close to serving time.

pizza puffs

2 sheets ready-rolled puff pastry

1 cup roasted red capsicum mayo
(page 211)

20 baby mozzarella balls
(bocconcini), halved and well
drained

1 tablespoons fresh oregano
leaves

2–3 slices prosciutto, cut into
small strips

10 pitted black olives, halved

olive oil

Preheat oven to 200°C. Line 2 baking trays with baking paper.

Cut small circles (about 5 cm across) from pastry and place on baking
tray. Spread with the capsicum mayo. Top half the pastry circles with
a mozzarella slice and 1 or 2 oregano leaves. Top the other circles with
prosciutto and olives (wind each strip of prosciutto to make a small 'twist',
then put half an olive in the centre) and drizzle with a few drops of olive oil.

Place trays in preheated oven and bake for 10–12 minutes or until pastry
is puffed. Serve hot or warm.

makes about 40

Prepare up to 1 day ahead; store (uncooked), covered, in fridge.

polenta & tapenade rounds

2 tablespoons butter

1 tablespoon olive oil

1 clove garlic, crushed

2 spring onions, finely sliced

300 ml boiling water

50 g instant polenta

100 g fetta cheese, crumbled

2 tablespoons chopped fresh oregano

salt and freshly ground black pepper

½ cup black-olive tapenade (page 210)

Lightly oil a 20-cm square baking dish.

Heat butter and olive oil in a non-stick saucepan over medium heat. When butter is melted, add garlic and spring onions and stir-fry for 5–6 minutes until softened. Pour in boiling water, then add polenta slowly in a thin stream, stirring constantly. Continue to cook, stirring, for about 5 minutes, until the mixture is smooth.

Remove from the heat, stir in fetta and oregano, and season with salt and pepper to taste. Pour polenta into prepared dish, smooth top, cover, and refrigerate overnight.

Preheat oven to 180°C. Lightly oil baking tray.

>

Use a biscuit cutter to cut polenta into small circles (or squares, if you prefer). Place on prepared baking tray, cover with aluminium foil and bake for 12–15 minutes until warmed through. Top each round with a small scoop of tapenade and serve warm.

makes 15–16

Polenta – cook up to 2 days ahead; refrigerate. Bring back to room temperature before reheating.

pork & pineapple skewers

400 g pork fillets, sliced into
strips 2 cm × 12 cm

2 cups cubed pineapple, fresh
or canned (drained)

24 bamboo skewers, soaked in
water for at least 30 minutes

1–2 tablespoons peanut oil

bought peanut (satay) sauce,
to serve

MARINADE

2 tablespoons tamari sauce
(see page 250)

1 tablespoon mirin (see page 249)

3 cloves garlic, crushed

1 teaspoon chilli oil

1 tablespoon caster sugar

½ teaspoon salt

Place all the marinade ingredients in a shallow bowl and mix until sugar
is dissolved. Add pork strips and marinate, turning occasionally, for 3–4
hours or overnight.

Thread pork strips lengthways onto skewers, pushing the meat together
to give a frilled effect, then finish with a pineapple cube.

Preheat grill or barbecue to high.

Brush prepared skewers lightly with oil and cook for about 3–4 minutes
on each side, or until browned. Serve immediately, with peanut sauce.

makes 24

⊙ Pork – marinate (in fridge) for up to 2 days ahead. Skewers – thread up
to 1 day ahead.

pork, prawn
& lemongrass wontons

350 g pork mince

150 g green (raw) prawns, peeled, deveined and finely chopped (or pulse in food processor)

1 × 225-g can water chestnuts, drained and finely chopped

1 tablespoon grated fresh ginger

2 tablespoons peeled and finely chopped lemongrass

1 teaspoon chilli jam

2 teaspoons soft brown sugar

2 egg yolks, beaten

1 packet wonton wrappers

chopped chives, to serve

SOY & GINGER DIPPING SAUCE

½ cup soy sauce

1 teaspoon sesame oil

½ teaspoon grated fresh ginger

½ teaspoon finely sliced fresh red chilli

To make dipping sauce, place all ingredients in a small bowl and whisk until combined. Set aside until needed.

To make wonton filling, place mince, prawns, water chestnuts, ginger, lemongrass, chilli jam, sugar and egg yolks in a bowl. Mix until combined.

Place 1 teaspoonful of the mixture in a centre of a wonton wrapper. Moisten edges with water, pull up sides to form a small bundle, twist, and press to keep together. (As you work, keep the wonton wrappers and wontons covered with a damp tea-towel to prevent them drying out.) Repeat with remaining mixture.

>

Place wontons on a tray, cover and refrigerate until ready to use.

Lightly oil the slats of a bamboo steamer or line with non-stick baking paper. Half-fill large saucepan or wok with boiling water. Place wontons in steamer (in 2 or 3 batches, depending on size of steamer), leaving some space between them. Place steamer over saucepan or wok, cover, and steam for 7–8 minutes until firm.

Transfer cooked wontons to a serving platter, sprinkle with chopped chives and serve immediately with the dipping sauce on the side.

makes 35–40

Dipping sauce – make 1 week ahead. Wontons – prepare up to 8 hours ahead; refrigerate uncooked.

Can freeze (uncooked) wontons for up to 4 weeks; defrost before steaming.

potato & rosemary mini pizzas

6 small ready-made pizza bases (about 12 cm in diameter)
6 chat potatoes (or small waxy potatoes)
2 sprigs rosemary
1–1½ tablespoons extra-virgin olive oil
salt and freshly ground black pepper

Preheat oven to 200°C. Lightly oil a baking tray.

Cut each pizza base into 6 triangles and place on prepared tray. Pull rosemary leaves from the stalks.

Slice potatoes as thinly as possible and place in a bowl with the oil, rosemary leaves, salt and pepper. Toss to coat.

Arrange potato slices, slightly overlapping, on the pizza bases, covering to the edges, then scatter with rosemary. Place in preheated oven and bake for 15 minutes until potatoes are soft but browned at the edges.

Serve immediately.

makes 36

Make up to 1 day ahead (but taste best if made close to serving). Reheat, covered with foil, in preheated 180°C oven for 10 minutes.

potato cakes with trout

500 g floury potatoes (e.g. sebago or King Edward), quartered

3 eggs, beaten

50 g self-raising flour, sifted

extra 2 egg whites, beaten to soft peaks

½ cup hot milk

salt and freshly ground black pepper

unsalted butter for frying

TOPPING

1 small smoked trout

¾ cup thick sour cream

2–3 tablespoons finely chopped fresh chives

freshly ground black pepper

Boil potatoes until soft, drain well and then mash. Place in a large bowl. When cold, beat in the eggs and flour until well mixed, then add milk and season with salt and pepper.

Stir about one-third of the beaten egg white into the mash, then gently fold in remainder.

Heat butter in large non-stick frying pan over medium heat. When butter is melted, drop in spoonfuls of the potatoe mix to make mini pancakes about 4 cm in diameter. Cook (in batches) for 3–4 minutes, turning once, until golden.

>

To prepare trout, peel off skin, break fish into bite-sized flakes and remove any tiny bones (use tweezers if necessary).

When pancakes are cool, top with a little sour cream, a piece of trout and a sprinkling of chives, and dust with freshly ground pepper.

makes about 20

Pancakes – make up to 2 days ahead; cover and refrigerate. Assemble up to 3 hours before serving.

prosciutto, pesto & rocket rolls

150 g ricotta
2 tablespoons pesto (page 216)
freshly ground black pepper
12 long slices prosciutto (or 24 small round slices)
½–1 cup rocket or baby spinach leaves

Mix ricotta with pesto and season with pepper.

Cut prosciutto slices in half. Spread each slice with some ricotta mix, then place a rocket (or spinach) leaf on top and roll up. Place join-side down on a serving platter.

makes 24

Ricotta–pesto mix – make up to 1 day ahead; refrigerate.
Rolls – assemble up to 2 hours ahead; cover and refrigerate.

pumpernickel with blue cheese & caramelised walnuts

6 slices pumpernickel bread

150 g soft blue cheese (e.g. Blue Castello)

vegetable oil (or vegetable oil spray)

24 walnut halves

½ cup caster sugar

2 tablespoons balsamic vinegar

Preheat oven to 180°C. Line a baking tray with non-stick baking paper.

To make caramelised walnuts, put sugar and vinegar in small saucepan over medium heat. Stir for about 3 minutes or until sugar dissolves. Add nuts and stir to coat, then put them in a single layer on prepared baking tray. Bake for about 10 minutes, until nuts are dark brown (watch carefully, as they will burn easily). Leave on tray to cool.

Cut each pumpernickel slice into 4 squares. Spread with the blue cheese and top with a caramelised walnut, then serve.

makes 24

Walnuts – caramelise up to 2 days ahead; store on non-stick paper in airtight container. Pumpernickel bites – spread with cheese up to 4 hours before serving; add walnuts close to serving time.

pumpkin pies

4 sheets ready-rolled shortcrust pastry

250 g pumpkin, peeled, cooked and mashed

2 rashers bacon, fried until crisp and then chopped

½–¾ cup grated tasty cheese

2 spring onions, finely chopped

2 tablespoons finely chopped flat-leaf parsley

2 eggs, separated

salt and freshly ground black pepper

1 beaten egg yolk, for glazing

Preheat oven to 200°C. Lightly grease 2 × 12-hole non-stick mini-muffin or small cupcake pans.

Cut pastry into 24 × 5-cm circles. Press half of the pastry circles into the muffin pans.

Place pumpkin, bacon, cheese, onion, parsley and egg yolks in a bowl and mix well.

Beat egg whites in a clean, dry bowl until stiff. Fold into the pumpkin mixture. Spoon mixture into patty pans (don't put too much in, as filling will puff up) and top with pastry lids.

Glaze tops with egg yolk and cut a slit for air to escape. Place in preheated oven and bake for 20–25 minutes until golden-brown.

Serve warm.

makes 24

Make pies up to 3 days ahead; refrigerate. Reheat in preheated 180°C oven for 15–30 minutes.

Can freeze baked pies for up to 1 month; cook from frozen, for 35–40 minutes.

quail eggs with
dukkah or nori flakes

6 cups water

1 tablespoon salt

1 teaspoon white vinegar

24 quail eggs

3 tablespoons nori flakes
(see page 249)

DUKKAH

4 tablespoons sesame seeds

2 tablespoons coriander seeds

1 tablespoon cumin seeds

1 teaspoon fennel seeds

1 teaspoon freshly ground black
pepper

1 teaspoon ground cinnamon

50 g dry-roasted hazelnuts

½ teaspoon salt flakes

To make dukkah, heat a small, heavy-based frying pan over high heat. Add sesame seeds and cook for a few minutes until lightly toasted. Tip into a bowl. Place coriander, cumin and fennel seeds, pepper and cinnamon into pan and cook for a few minutes until they start to toast and release their fragrance. Add to sesame seeds.

Put hazelnuts in blender and pulse until crushed but still with some texture. Put all the prepared seeds and spices in a spice grinder and pulse to a coarse powder, then mix with the hazelnuts and salt flakes. When completely cold, store in an airtight container until needed.

>

To cook the eggs, bring water, salt and vinegar to the boil in a medium–large saucepan over high heat. Add eggs and boil for 3 minutes. Remove eggs and place in cold water to stop cooking. When cool, peel off shells.

Pile eggs into a bowl, and put dukkah and nori flakes into separate bowls, so guests can dip the eggs into either. Or, if preferred, dip 12 eggs into dukkah and 12 eggs into nori flakes, and then serve.

makes 24

Eggs – boil and peel up to 2 days ahead; store, well covered, in fridge. Dukkah – make up to 4 weeks ahead (though will lose some of its fresh flavour); store in sealed jar.

risotto balls with basil & bocconcini

4 cups vegetable stock

2 tablespoons olive oil

1 onion, finely sliced

1 cup arborio (or other risotto) rice

2 cups peeled, diced tomatoes

1 tablespoon butter

¾ cup freshly grated parmesan cheese

salt and freshly ground black pepper

200 g baby mozzarella balls (bocconcini), diced

1 tablespoon chopped fresh basil

plain flour for dusting

2 eggs, beaten

1 cup dried breadcrumbs

extra olive or vegetable oil

Heat vegetable stock and keep warm.

Heat oil in a large non-stick saucepan over medium heat. Stir-fry onion for 3–4 minutes until soft but not browned. Reduce heat, add rice and tomato, then stir for 2–3 minutes until rice is coated and tomato softened.

Add a ladleful of hot stock to the rice and stir until it is absorbed. Continue adding stock in small amounts for about 20 minutes, stirring until all stock is used and rice is cooked (it should be soft but *al dente* – with a slight bite). When cooked, stir in the butter and parmesan cheese, and season to taste with salt and freshly ground pepper. Allow to cool.

>

Stir the bocconcini and basil through the cooled rice, and use wet hands to shape mixture into small balls. Dip into flour, then egg, then breadcrumbs and press lightly to coat. Place in fridge for at least 15 minutes.

Put enough of the extra oil in a large frying pan to shallow-fry the risotto balls, and place over medium heat. When oil is hot, fry risotto balls in several batches until golden. Drain on crumpled kitchen paper and serve hot or at room temperature.

makes 25–30

Make up to 5 days ahead; refrigerate. Reheat, covered with foil, in preheated 180°C oven for 15–20 minutes.

roast beef & wasabi crostini

12 small slices (about 1.5 cm
thick) ciabatta bread

olive oil for brushing

2 cloves garlic, halved

¼ cup thick sour cream

1 teaspoon wasabi paste

250 g rare roast beef, thinly sliced

watercress or rocket leaves,
to serve

Preheat oven to 200°C.

Brush ciabatta slices lightly with oil, rub one side with cut garlic, place
on baking sheet and bake for 10–15 minutes until crisp and golden-brown.
Leave to cool.

Combine sour cream and wasabi paste, and mix well.

Place crostini on a platter. Top with 1 or 2 watercress or rocket leaves,
a slice of beef and a small dollop of wasabi cream, and serve.

makes 12

Toasts – make 1 week ahead; store in airtight container. Assemble
crostini 3–4 hours before serving.

roman summer skewers

20 baby mozzarella balls
(bocconcini)

2 tablespoons extra-virgin
olive oil

1 tablespoon pesto (page 216)

40 small fresh basil leaves

20 cherry tomatoes

20 pitted black olives

20 cocktail sticks

Drain bocconcini and place in a bowl with the olive oil and pesto. Stir until coated, cover, and marinate for 15–20 minutes.

Thread bocconcini, with a tomato, an olive and 2 basil leaves, onto each cocktail stick. Arrange on a platter and serve.

makes 20

Bocconcini – marinate in fridge up to a day ahead. Skewers – thread up to 2 hours before serving; keep refrigerated. If making them further ahead, omit basil leaves, which wilt quickly.

san choy bao

1 tablespoon sunflower oil

1 clove garlic, crushed

2 spring onions, chopped

1 teaspoon finely grated fresh ginger

1 tablespoon sesame seeds

½ cup canned water chestnuts, drained and chopped

500 g pork mince

1 tablespoon kecap manis (sweet soy sauce – see page 249)

2 tablespoons oyster sauce

16 baby cos lettuce leaves

extra 2 spring onions, finely sliced on an angle

Heat oil over medium–high heat in a non-stick frying pan or wok. Add garlic, spring onions, ginger and sesame seeds, and fry for 1–2 minutes until fragrance is released. Add water chestnuts and pork mince, and stir-fry until mince is well browned (about 4–5 minutes). Add kecap manis and oyster sauce, reduce heat and simmer for 5 minutes.

Trim lettuce leaves if necessary to get an even size. Arrange lettuce 'cups' on a platter and spoon in the mince. Sprinkle with a little spring onion and serve immediately.

makes 16

Filling – make 2 days ahead; refrigerate. Reheat in frying pan, or in (covered) casserole in preheated 180°C oven for 10–15 minutes. Lettuce cups – fill just before serving.

satay chicken
with spicy peanut sauce

12 chicken tenderloins, cut in half lengthways

24 bamboo skewers, soaked in water for 30 minutes

lime wedges

1 cup bought peanut (satay) sauce

2 tablespoons freshly squeezed lime juice

3 spring onions, chopped

1 stalk lemongrass, peeled and chopped

1 teaspoon brown sugar

1 teaspoon ground cumin

1 teaspoon ground coriander

1 tablespoon peanut oil

1 tablespoons soy sauce

To make marinade, mix all ingredients in a bowl. Add the chicken and stir to coat. Cover, and marinate in fridge for 30–60 minutes.

Preheat grill or barbecue to medium–high. Cook chicken for 5–6 minutes, turning several times, until cooked.

Place peanut sauce and lime juice in a small saucepan over medium heat, and stir until mixed. Serve satay with warm peanut sauce, and lime wedges.

makes 24

Chicken – marinate up to 2 days ahead.

scallops with orange zest & vermouth

1 kg scallops off the shell, roe removed

salt and freshly ground black pepper

2 tablespoons peanut oil

3 tablespoons butter

2 spring onions, finely sliced

½ cup dry vermouth

1 teaspoon grated orange zest

Pat scallops dry and season lightly with salt and pepper.

Heat 1 tablespoon of the oil in a large non-stick frying pan over medium heat. When oil is hot, add half the scallops and sear for 1–2 minutes, turning once, until browned on both sides (be careful not to overcook, or they will be tough). Transfer to a plate and keep warm. Add remaining oil and scallops, and cook the second batch. Keep scallops warm.

Wipe out pan, add butter and melt over medium heat. Add spring onions and sauté for 1 minute. Add vermouth and orange zest and cook, stirring, for 1–2 minutes until sauce thickens. Return scallops to pan for about 1 minute and stir gently.

Place scallops in shells, glasses, or Chinese spoons, with a little sauce, and serve immediately.

makes about 30

scallops with wakame & ginger

75 g dried wakame flakes
(see page 250)

2 teaspoons mirin

24 scallops off the shell, roe
removed

salt and freshly ground black
pepper

2–3 tablespoons vegetable oil

about ½ cup pickled ginger,
finely sliced, to serve

1 tablespoon sesame oil

3 tablespoons toasted sesame
seeds, to serve

Put wakame flakes in a small bowl, add mirin and enough boiling water to cover. Leave for 7–8 minutes to soak. Drain, pressing lightly to remove excess liquid.

Rinse scallops, pat dry and season with salt and pepper. Heat 1 tablespoon vegetable oil in a large frying pan over medium–high heat. Sear scallops in 2 or 3 batches for about 1 minute (depending on size, but be careful not to overcook, or they will be tough). Add more oil as needed.

Serve seared scallops on shells or in Chinese spoons. Top with a pinch of wakame and a curl of pickled ginger. Drizzle with 1–2 drops of sesame oil, sprinkle with sesame seeds and serve immediately.

makes 24

sesame-crusted prawns
with lime dipping sauce

1 tablespoon sunflower or vegetable oil

salt and freshly ground black pepper

20 medium-sized green (raw) prawns, peeled and deveined but tails left intact

2 tablespoons sesame seeds

LIME-ZEST DIPPING SAUCE

1 cup mayonnaise (page 211)

1 teaspoon finely grated lime zest

2 teaspoons freshly squeezed lime juice

1 teaspoon finely chopped fresh coriander

To make the dipping sauce, combine all the ingredients in a bowl and stir until mixed. Cover, and refrigerate for at least 30 minutes before serving.

Preheat oven to 220°C. Line a baking tray with aluminium foil.

Put oil, salt and pepper in a large bowl. Add prawns and toss to coat. Place sesame seeds on a plate, dip one side of each prawn into the seeds and press lightly. Place prawns on prepared baking tray, seeds facing up. Place in preheated oven and bake for 6–7 minutes.

Arrange on a platter and serve with dipping sauce and plenty of napkins.

makes 20

Dipping sauce – make up to 2 days ahead; refrigerate. Prawns – coat up to 6 hours ahead; refrigerate. Cook just before serving.

shanghai chicken dumplings

3 dried shiitake mushrooms

250 g chicken mince

2 water chestnuts (drain if canned), finely chopped

3 tablespoons finely sliced spring onion

1 tablespoon grated fresh ginger

1 clove garlic, crushed

1 tablespoon finely sliced fresh red chilli

1 tablespoon soy sauce

1 teaspoon sesame oil

salt and white pepper

25 round gow-gee wrappers

DIPPING SAUCE

½ cup soy sauce

2 tablespoons mirin (rice wine – see page 249), or dry sherry

1 teaspoon sesame oil

1 teaspoon finely grated ginger

To make dipping sauce, combine all ingredients in a small bowl and stir until mixed. Cover and set aside until needed.

Put dried mushrooms in a small bowl, cover with boiling water and soak for 15 minutes. Drain, squeeze out any excess moisture and chop flesh finely (if stalks are tough, remove and discard).

Place chicken, water chestnuts, spring onions, ginger, garlic, chilli, soy, sesame oil, salt and pepper in a bowl, and mix until combined. Cover and refrigerate for at least 30 minutes.

>

Place a small spoonful of the chicken mixture in the centre of a gow-gee wrapper. Moisten edges with water and fold over into a semi-circle. Pinch the edges together, then stand the dumpling on its base with the frill at the top. Keep wrappers and finished dumplings under a damp tea-towel as you work, to avoid them drying out.

Lightly oil the base of a large bamboo steamer. Half fill wok or pot with boiling water, place dumplings in steamer (in batches) and steam for 7–8 minutes. Remove, and serve with the dipping sauce.

makes 25

Filling – make up to 3 days ahead; refrigerate. Dumplings – assemble up to 8 hours ahead; steam just before serving.

Can freeze uncooked dumplings for up to 1 month; defrost before steaming.

skewered salmon
with a marmalade glaze

750 g salmon fillets, skin and any
bones removed

20 bamboo skewers, soaked in
water for at least 30 minutes

lime wedges, to serve

MARMALADE GLAZE

½ cup orange marmalade

1 tablespoon cranberry sauce

½ cup orange juice

1 tablespoon Dijon mustard

First make the marmalade glaze: put all the ingredients in a small saucepan
over medium heat and simmer for about 10 minutes, until reduced. Leave
to cool.

Preheat oven or barbecue grill to medium.

Cut fish into 2-cm cubes and then thread onto skewers. Brush with the
glaze and grill skewers for about 1–2 minutes on each side or until cooked
as you like it. Serve hot, or at room temperature, with lime wedges.

makes 20

Glaze – make up to 3 days ahead. Skewers – thread up to 1 day ahead,
or grill several hours ahead and serve at room temperature.

smoked-salmon & chive parcels

150 g cream cheese
1 teaspoon finely grated lemon zest
2 teaspoons green peppercorns, drained and lightly crushed
2 tablespoons chopped chives
12 slices smoked salmon
extra small bunch of chives

Put cream cheese, lemon zest, peppercorns and herbs in a bowl and mix well. Refrigerate for at least 30 minutes.

Place a spoonful of the cheese mixture in the centre of a salmon slice, and fold sides over to form a small parcel. Wrap a chive around the parcel and tie with a knot. Place, join-side down, on a platter and refrigerate for 30 minutes, or until cheese is firm.

Serve chilled.

makes 12

Make up to 1 day ahead; keep covered in fridge.

smoked-trout
pâté with french toasts

½ French bread stick (baguette),
cut into 1-cm slices

1 small smoked trout (about 375 g)

100 g cream cheese

1–2 tablespoons freshly squeezed
lemon juice

2 tablespoons finely chopped
fresh dill

pinch of ground cayenne

freshly ground black pepper

extra fresh dill, for garnish

Preheat oven to 150°C.

To make French toasts, lay bread slices on a baking tray, place in preheated oven and bake for 20 minutes or until quite dry (they may start to curl, but this is fine). Allow to cool completely.

To make the pâté, remove skin and all bones (use tweezers if necessary) from the fish. Place flesh in blender or food processor with the other ingredients (except the extra dill) and blend until smooth. Spoon into a bowl, cover and refrigerate or at least 30 minutes, or until ready to serve.

Serve pâté in a bowl with fresh dill on top. Pile toasts onto a plate and allow guests to spread their own.

makes about 24

Toasts – make up to 2 weeks ahead; store in airtight container.
Pâté – make up to 5 days ahead; store covered in fridge.

spiced mixed nuts

1 tablespoon butter

1 tablespoon olive oil

3 cups raw mixed nuts
(e.g. almonds, cashews and
peanuts)

2–3 tablespoons salt flakes

1 teaspoon ground cumin

1 teaspoon mild ground chilli

1 teaspoon ground sweet paprika

Heat butter and oil in a heavy-based frying pan over medium heat. Add nuts and stir until coated, then stir-fry until nuts are toasted and golden-brown. Tip into a bowl, add salt and spices, and stir until well mixed.

Serve warm or cold.

makes 3 cups

Make up to a week ahead; store in airtight container.

spicy lamb skewers
with saffron dip

450 g lamb fillets, roughly chopped

1 red onion, finely chopped

2 tablespoons very finely chopped peanuts

about 20 bamboo skewers, soaked in water for at least 30 minutes

MARINADE

1½ cups Greek-style yoghurt

1 tablespoon vegetable oil

2 cloves garlic, crushed

1 tablespoon chopped fresh coriander

2 tablespoons freshly squeezed lemon juice

1 teaspoon garam masala (see page 248)

½ teaspoon ground paprika

½ teaspoon ground cardamom

SAFFRON DIP

generous pinch of saffron threads

1 tablespoon boiling water

1 tablespoon freshly squeezed lemon juice

1 cup Greek-style yoghurt

pinch of salt

To make the dip, put the saffron threads in a small bowl, cover with boiling water and leave for a few minutes to dissolve. Stir saffron water and lemon juice into the yoghurt, and mix. Season with salt to taste, cover, and refrigerate for at least 30 minutes or until needed.

To make the marinade, mix all the ingredients together in a bowl.

>

Put lamb in a food processor or blender with the onion and peanuts, and pulse until the meat is finely chopped. Add 2 tablespoons of the marinade and blend until mixed, and firm enough to hold together. Shape mixture into small egg-shaped patties about 4-cm long. Place in a single layer in a shallow dish, spoon marinade over, cover, and refrigerate overnight.

Preheat oven grill to medium–high. Line a baking tray with aluminium foil.

Thread one patty onto each skewer and arrange on prepared baking tray. Grill for about 5–6 minutes, turning until cooked through and golden-brown.

Arrange on a platter and serve hot with saffron dip in a bowl or bowls.

makes about 20

Dip – make up to 3 days ahead. Lamb patties – can be cooked up to 3 days ahead (but do not marinate for more than 1 night as mixture will become soggy). Reheat in a single layer, covered with foil, in preheated 180°C oven for about 10 minutes.

spicy thai cashews

2 cups raw cashews

2 tablespoons peanut or sunflower oil

1 teaspoon dried chilli flakes

¼ cup caster sugar

¼ teaspoon sea salt

Preheat oven to 180°C. Line a baking tray with non-stick baking paper.

Spread cashews on baking tray, place in preheated oven and bake for 20–30 minutes, turning once or twice, until golden. Remove from oven, transfer to a plate and allow to cool.

Pour the oil into a large non-stick frying pan. Add chilli flakes and heat over medium–high heat. When oil is hot, add nuts and stir-fry for about 30 seconds. Add salt and sugar, and stir-fry for about 1 minute (take care they don't burn). Remove from heat and transfer to a plate to cool.

Serve warm or at room temperature.

makes 2 cups

Make up to 1 week ahead; store in airtight jar.

spiky filo tarts of crab & mayo

200 g filo pastry

110 g butter, melted

CRAB & MAYO FILLING

200 g fresh crab meat, flaked

juice and zest of 1 lemon

2 sticks celery, finely sliced

4 tablespoons mayonnaise (page 211)

salt and freshly ground black pepper

1 tablespoon chopped fresh chives, to serve

Preheat oven to 180°C. Lightly butter 2 × 12-hole mini-muffin or cupcake pans.

Lay one sheet of pastry on a flat surface and brush with melted butter. Lay another sheet on top and brush with butter, then repeat with another sheet. (While you are working, keep the unused filo covered with a damp tea-towel.) Cut pastry into small squares about 6 cm × 6 cm (or to fit your muffin tin), and place in the muffin tins, arranging the squares at slightly different angles to create a 'spiky' edge.

Place tray in preheated oven and bake for 6–7 minutes, until cases are crisp and golden. Remove from oven and cool tarts on a cake rack.

To make filling, mix crab meat, lemon, juice and zest, celery and mayo in a bowl. Season to taste with salt and pepper. Keep refrigerated until ready to serve.

To serve, spoon filling into filo cases, piling it into a small mound, and scatter with a few chives. Arrange on a platter and serve immediately.

makes about 20

Filo cases – bake up to 1 week ahead; store in airtight container. Filling – make up to 1 day ahead; store covered in fridge. Assemble tarts as close to serving time as possible.

spinach, bacon & cheese balls

1 bunch spinach, leaves very
finely chopped

4 rashers bacon, fried until crisp,
then crumbled

100 g Swiss cheese, grated

100 g parmesan cheese, freshly
grated

2 eggs

freshly ground black pepper

¾ cup dried breadcrumbs

2 tablespoons sesame seeds

¾ cup plain flour

1 egg, lightly beaten, for dipping

vegetable oil for deep-frying

Place spinach, bacon, cheeses, one of the eggs (lightly beaten), and the pepper in a bowl and mix well. Shape into small balls.

Mix the breadcrumbs with the sesame seeds, season with salt and extra pepper, and place on a plate. Dip the spinach balls into the flour and shake off any excess, then dip into the other egg (also lightly beaten), and finally into the breadcrumb mix.

Heat oil in a deep pan until hot. Fry spinach balls in batches until lightly golden-brown. Drain on crumpled kitchen paper and serve warm.

makes 30

Cook up to 3 days ahead; refrigerate. Reheat, covered with foil, in preheated 180°C oven for 10–15 minutes.

sushi rolls

400 g sushi rice

2 avocados

5–6 sheets nori (see page 249)

2 Lebanese cucumbers, cut into long strips

freshly squeezed lemon juice

1 small red capsicum, cut into thin strips

2 tablespoons toasted sesame seeds

soy sauce, wasabi paste and pickled ginger, to serve

4 tablespoons rice vinegar

2 tablespoons caster sugar

1 teaspoon salt

To prepare the sushi dressing, heat the vinegar, sugar and salt over a low heat until sugar has dissolved. Leave to cool.

Meanwhile, put the rice in a sieve and wash under cold water until water runs clear. Drain well (if you have time, leave it to drain for an hour), then put into a medium-size saucepan with 2 cups of cold water. Bring to the boil, cover, reduce heat and simmer for 15 minutes. Remove from heat and leave, with lid on, to steam for 10–15 minutes.

Tip the cooked rice into a large, flat-based dish or baking tray and spread out. Sprinkle gradually with the prepared dressing, using a spatula to turn the rice, until it has cooled to room temperature. Cover with a clean, damp cloth until ready to use.

Cut the avocados into long thin strips and sprinkle with lemon juice to stop the flesh discolouring.

Lay one sheet of nori on a bamboo sushi-rolling mat. Spread rice over two-thirds of the nori (starting at the edge closest to you) using your fingers to spread rice evenly. Sprinkle with some sesame seeds, then top with a strip each of cucumber, avocado and capsicum. Use the bamboo mat to roll up the nori sheet, holding the filling tightly in place. When you have almost finished rolling, moisten the long edge of the nori sheet with water and press firmly to seal.

Set the completed roll aside, covered with damp cloth or in an airtight container. Repeat process with the remaining nori sheets.

When ready to serve, trim the ends and cut each roll into about 10 slices, using a very sharp knife. Arrange on tray with separate bowls for the soy sauce, wasabi and pickled ginger.

makes about 50

Make several hours ahead, but slice just before serving.

thai chicken & coconut pies

1 tablespoon vegetable oil

350 g chicken mince

1 clove garlic, crushed

4 tablespoons coconut milk

2 tablespoons sweet chilli sauce

2 teaspoons lemongrass, peeled and finely chopped

1 tablespoon freshly squeezed lime juice

1 teaspoon finely grated lime zest

2 tablespoons finely chopped fresh coriander

4 sheets ready-rolled puff pastry

1 egg, lightly beaten, to glaze

1 tablespoon sesame seeds

Heat oil in a large, non-stick frying pan over medium. Add chicken mince and cook, stirring, for 6–7 minutes until lightly browned. Cool.

Combine chicken with the garlic, coconut milk, chilli sauce, lemongrass, lime juice and zest, and coriander. Mix well, cover, and refrigerate for at least 15 minutes.

Preheat oven to 220°C. Lightly oil a non-stick, 12-hole muffin pan.

Cut 12 rounds of pastry 8.5 cm wide, and 12 rounds 6.5 cm wide. Fit larger rounds into muffin holes and press lightly. Fill each pastry cup with chicken mixture, then top with smaller round, pressing edges to seal.

Brush pies with egg to glaze, cut a small slit in the centre of lid, and sprinkle with sesame seeds. Place in preheated oven and bake for 25 minutes, or until golden-brown and puffed on top.

Serve hot or warm.

makes 12

Bake up to 2 days ahead; reheat in preheated 180°C oven for 10–15 minutes.

Can freeze pies (baked or unbaked) for up to 2 months; cook from frozen, for 30–35 minutes.

thai fish cakes
with sweet & sour sauce

400 g boneless white fish fillets (e.g. flathead or ling)

1 tablespoon freshly squeezed lime juice

1 tablespoon fish sauce (nam pla)

1 clove garlic, crushed

1 tablespoon grated fresh ginger

2 kaffir lime leaves, finely sliced

1 tablespoon finely sliced fresh red chilli

2 spring onions, finely sliced

2 tablespoons chopped fresh coriander

½ cup finely sliced green beans

1 cup dried breadcrumbs

peanut oil for shallow frying

SWEET & SOUR SAUCE

2 tablespoons freshly squeezed lime juice

1 tablespoon rice vinegar

2 tablespoons fish sauce (nam pla – see page 249)

3 tablespoons water

2 teaspoons caster sugar

a few drops chilli oil

2 tablespoons finely grated carrot

a few fresh coriander leaves

To make sauce, put all ingredients except coriander into a small bowl and whisk until mixed. Stir in the coriander and cover until ready to serve.

Place fish, lime juice, fish sauce, garlic, ginger, lime leaves and chilli in a food processer or blender, and blend until combined. Tip mixture into a large bowl, then add the spring onions, coriander, beans and breadcrumbs and stir until mixed.

>

Shape mixture into small patties about 3–4 cm in diameter. Heat oil in a large non-stick frying pan over medium heat, then fry fish cakes in batches until golden-brown on both sides and cooked through. Drain on kitchen paper.

Serve hot or warm, with the sweet & sour sauce for dipping.

makes about 24

Sauce – make up to 3 days ahead, but add coriander close to serving time. Fish cakes – prepare 1 day ahead; keep (uncooked) covered in fridge and fry just before serving.

thyme cheese twists

2 egg yolks
1 tablespoon Dijon mustard
2 sheets ready-rolled puff pastry
2 tablespoons fresh thyme leaves
100 g grated Swiss cheese
2 tablespoons freshly grated parmesan cheese

Preheat oven to 180°C. Line a large baking tray with non-stick baking paper.

Whisk 1 egg yolk with mustard and use a pastry brush to spread it evenly over pastry sheets. Sprinkle thyme leaves and cheeses over pastry and press in lightly.

Cut pastry sheets in half, then into 2-cm wide strips. Twist each strip fairly tightly and place on prepared baking tray. Beat the remaining egg yolk and brush over twists. Bake in preheated oven for 12–15 minutes, or until puffed and golden. Cool on a cooling rack. Serve warm or at room temperature.

makes 24

Prepare twists 1 day ahead; refrigerate unbaked. Or bake 1 day ahead and store in an airtight container at room temperature.

Freeze (uncooked) for up to 2 months; bake from frozen, for 15–20 minutes.

tiny caesar salad tarts

24 ready-made cocktail tart cases

2 slices prosciutto

2 tablespoons mayonnaise
(page 211)

1 clove garlic, crushed

1 teaspoon freshly squeezed
lemon juice

2 anchovy fillets, mashed

2 tablespoons grated parmesan
cheese

freshly ground black pepper

1 baby cos lettuce, leaves finely
shredded

2 tablespoons chopped chives,
to serve

Preheat oven to 200°C.

Place prosciutto on a non-stick baking tray and bake in oven for 10 minutes until crisp. Break into small pieces.

Place mayonnaise, garlic, lemon juice, anchovy fillets, parmesan and pepper in a bowl and whisk until combined.

Fill each tart case with shredded lettuce, drizzle some dressing over, top with some prosciutto and a few chives, then serve.

makes 24

Dressing – make 1 day ahead. Tarts – fill just before serving.

trout rice-paper rolls
with lime & ginger sauce

500 g trout fillets, 2–3 cm thick, skinned and deboned

12 rice-paper sheets (see page 249)

½ cup fresh coriander leaves

2 spring onions, finely chopped

12 Vietnamese mint leaves

MARINADE

5 tablespoons freshly squeezed lemon juice

2 tablespoons chopped fresh coriander leaves

1 teaspoon finely grated fresh ginger

salt and freshly ground black pepper

LIME & GINGER DIPPING SAUCE

6 tablespoons freshly squeezed lime juice

1 tablespoon rice wine vinegar

2 teaspoons soy sauce

2 teaspoons caster sugar

2 teaspoon grated fresh ginger

Place the marinade ingredients in a shallow bowl and mix to combine. Cut the trout fillets into strips, and place in single layer in the marinade. Cover, and leave for 30–40 minutes, turning once or twice.

To make the dipping sauce, combine all ingredients except coriander leaves, and mix well. Set aside.

Preheat oven grill to medium–high and grill the fish pieces for 4–5 minutes until cooked, basting with the marinade. Remove from heat and allow to cool.

>

Soak 1 sheet of rice paper in warm water, then place on clean work surface and wait until soft enough to roll (20–30 seconds). Working quickly, place some coriander leaves near one edge of the rice paper. Top with a piece of fish, some spring onion, a mint leaf and some more coriander leaves. Roll up, tucking in the ends to make a small parcel. Place on a flat dish and cover with a damp towel while you make up the remainder of rolls.

Cover assembled rolls with plastic wrap and keep refrigerated until time to serve.

Serve with lime & ginger dipping sauce.

makes 12

Fish – marinate and cook 1 day ahead; keep refrigerated. Sauce – make up to 3 days ahead. Assemble rolls up to 5 hours ahead (keep well covered), though they are best made close to serving time.

warm roasted olives

500 g good-quality black and green olives in brine
4 cloves garlic, crushed
1 tablespoon chopped fresh oregano
½ teaspoon dried chilli flakes
zest of ½ lemon, cut into long strips
2–3 tablespoons extra-virgin olive oil

Preheat oven to 200°C.

Place olives in a bowl with the other ingredients and toss until olives are coated with oil. Tip into a shallow baking dish, place in preheated oven and roast for 15 minutes.

Serve warm.

makes about 2½ cups

Marinate olives up to 2 weeks ahead; roast just before serving.

sweet bites

Small *and* sweet: these delicate-looking, delicious-tasting treats are just right for an afternoon-tea party, or to serve near the end of a cocktail party.

Unless you are catering for a huge crowd, two or three varieties are usually plenty (if you are not sure what to choose, serve something chocolatey – you can hardly go wrong).

This section also includes some larger cakes and desserts, suitable for a sit-down dinner or buffet-style party. A luscious chocolate cake, a generous bowl of tiramisu dredged in cocoa, or delicately scented vanilla-poached fruits are always more than welcome.

< caramelised fruit kebabs (page 182)

caramelised fruit kebabs

16 bamboo skewers, soaked in water for at least 30 minutes

1 small pineapple, peeled, quartered and cored

3 punnets medium-sized strawberries, hulled

2 teaspoons balsamic vinegar

2 tablespoons caster sugar

Preheat oven grill or barbecue to high.

Cut pineapple quarters into small triangles. Thread, alternating with the strawberries, onto skewers. Grill for 2 minutes, then sprinkle with balsamic and sugar and grill for a further 2–3 minutes until fruit is caramelised.

Serve immediately.

makes 16

Skewers – thread up to 4 hours ahead; refrigerate covered. Grill just before serving.

chocolate & walnut macaroons

250 g good-quality dark chocolate, chopped

3 egg whites

pinch of salt

150 g caster sugar

1 teaspoon vanilla extract

165 g shredded coconut

60 g toasted, chopped walnuts

Preheat oven to 165°C. Line a baking tray with non-stick baking paper.

Put chocolate in a heatproof bowl over a pan of simmering water (make sure the bottom of the bowl does not touch the water). Stir until chocolate is melted, then leave to cool.

Put egg whites and salt in a clean dry bowl and whisk until foamy. Gradually add sugar and keep whisking until whites hold peaks. Stir in vanilla extract, then fold in the melted chocolate, the coconut and the walnuts. Use a teaspoon to drop small mounds of the mixture onto prepared tray. Place in preheated oven and bake for 10–12 minutes.

Leave the cooked macaroons on tray for a few minutes, then transfer to a cooling rack. They should be lightly crisp on the outside and soft inside.

makes 30

Bake up to 3 days ahead; keep in airtight container.

chocolate-dipped strawberries

500 g strawberries (they need to be perfect)
50 g dark chocolate, chopped
50 g white chocolate, chopped

Wipe strawberries clean, leaving hulls intact. Divide strawberries into two batches.

Place a sheet of non-stick baking paper on a baking tray or flat dish.

Put dark chocolate in a heatproof bowl over a pan of gently simmering water (make sure the bottom of the bowl does not touch the water, and don't let any steam or water drops touch the chocolate). When chocolate is melted, dip the first batch of strawberries into the chocolate one at a time, holding the stalk, and cover half the fruit. Lay on the baking paper to set.

Melt white chocolate in a bowl (as above) then dip the second batch of strawberries into white chocolate, coating just one half.

Allow about 1 hour for chocolate to set. Arrange on a platter to serve.

makes about 20 (depending on size of strawberries)

Best made within a few hours of serving; keep in a cool place, or covered in fridge.

coffee meringues
with raspberry cream

3 egg whites

2 pinches cream of tartar

225 g caster sugar

½ teaspoon instant coffee powder

RASPBERRY CREAM

¾ cup double cream

½ teaspoon vanilla extract

1 tablespoon caster sugar

¾ cup Greek-style yoghurt

½ cup raspberries, lightly crushed

Preheat oven to 120°C. Line 2 baking trays with non-stick baking paper.

Put egg whites into a clean, dry bowl and whisk on low speed with an electric mixer until frothy. Add cream of tartar and beat on high speed until mixture holds its shape in peaks. Add 2 tablespoons of sugar and beat for a further 2 minutes (mixture will start to become glossy). Add remaining sugar and the coffee powder, and beat until just mixed.

Pipe or spoon mixture into small, even-shaped rounds on the prepared trays. Place in preheated oven and bake for 1½ hours. Turn off oven, leave door ajar and leave meringues in oven until completely cool. Then remove from oven and store in an airtight container until needed.

To make raspberry cream, whip cream with vanilla extract and sugar until mixture holds its shape. Fold in yoghurt, then swirl the mixture through the crushed raspberries. Cover, and refrigerate until needed.

>

When ready to serve, join pairs of meringues with raspberry cream. Arrange on serving platter, and serve immediately.

makes 20–24

Meringues – cook 1 week ahead; store in airtight container. Raspberry cream – make 1 day ahead. Assemble meringues just before serving.

flourless chocolate almond cake

400 g good-quality dark
chocolate, chopped

250 g butter, melted

3 tablespoons warm water

4 tablespoons coffee liqueur
(e.g. Tia Maria)

6 eggs, separated

225 g caster sugar

240 g ground almonds

CHOCOLATE CREAM GLAZE

220 g dark chocolate

1 cup thickened cream

Preheat oven to 180°C. Lightly grease a 23-cm cake pan and line with non-stick baking paper.

Put chocolate in a heatproof bowl over a pan of simmering water (make sure bowl does not touch water) and stir until melted. Put chocolate, butter, water and coffee liqueur into a large bowl and stir to combine.

Beat eggs yolks and sugar with an electric mixer until pale and fluffy. Put egg whites in a clean, dry bowl and beat until soft peaks form.

Fold egg yolks and almonds gradually into the chocolate mixture, then fold in egg whites. Pour into prepared cake pan, place in preheated oven and bake for 1¼ hours.

>

Allow cake to cool in pan before inverting onto a rack to cool. When cake is cool, refrigerate for 30 minutes before glazing.

To make glaze, melt chocolate (as above). Leave to cool a little, then mix with the cream until smooth. Pour over the chilled cake, allowing glaze to run down sides and create a smooth finish.

serves 10–12

Bake and glaze cake up to 3 days ahead; keep covered in fridge.

greek shortbread crescents

125 g blanched almonds, lightly toasted

250 g butter, at room temperature

185 g icing sugar

1 tablespoon rosewater

1 teaspoon finely grated lemon zest

300 g plain flour, sifted

Preheat oven to 180°C. Line a baking tray with non-stick baking paper.

Chop almonds with a sharp knife, or pulse briefly in a blender or food processor.

Beat butter and 4 tablespoons icing sugar until pale and creamy. Add rosewater and lemon zest, and beat in.

Mix the flour with the chopped almonds. Gently fold dry ingredients into the butter mixture to make a light dough. Roll the dough into small balls, then form into crescent shapes and place on prepared baking tray. (If the dough is quite soft, dust your hands with a little plain flour as you are making them.) Bake in preheated oven for 15–20 minutes or until pale gold, then transfer to a cooling rack.

>

When completely cool, dredge shortbreads generously with the remaining icing sugar.

makes about 36

Make up to 1 week ahead; store in airtight container.

orange chocolate truffles

350 g good-quality dark chocolate, chopped

75 g caster sugar

250 g unsalted butter, at room temperature, chopped

3 egg yolks, lightly beaten

1 teaspoon very finely grated orange zest

2 teaspoons orange liqueur (e.g. Grand Marnier)

cocoa powder, or finely chopped almonds or pistachios, to coat

Put chocolate, sugar and butter into a heatproof bowl over a pan of simmering water and leave till melted, stirring occasionally. Allow to cool a little, then beat in the egg yolks and stir in the orange zest and liqueur.

Set aside in a cool place (refrigerate in very hot weather) for 4–5 hours, until mixture is stiff. Shape into small balls, roll these in the cocoa or chopped nuts, then place on a tray lined with non-stick baking paper. Refrigerate until needed.

For a luxurious effect, serve truffles in gold-foil cases (available from specialist food suppliers).

makes 20–30

Make 2–3 days ahead; store, covered, in fridge or cool place.

pear & vanilla upside-down cake

6 cups water

250 g caster sugar

1 vanilla bean, split

1 kg just-ripe pears, peeled and halved

200 g butter, at room temperature

175 g sugar

2 eggs, lightly beaten

410 g self-raising flour, sifted

160 ml full-cream milk

double cream, to serve

Put water, sugar and vanilla bean in a wide saucepan or frying pan over medium heat and bring to a simmer. Stir until sugar in dissolved, then add pears and simmer for 10–15 minutes, until pears are cooked but still holding their shape. Remove from poaching liquid and leave to drain (you need them as dry as possible). Remove vanilla bean, scrape out any remaining seeds and set these aside.

Preheat oven to 175°C. Lightly grease a 28-cm round springform cake pan and line with non-stick baking paper.

When pears have cooled, finely chop 2 of the halves. Arrange the other halves carefully over the base of cake pan, then top with the finely chopped pear (to fill in any gaps).

Beat butter with sugar until pale and fluffy. Add eggs gradually, contining to beat. Add flour and milk alternately, a little at a time. Finally, stir through the vanilla seeds. Spoon batter carefully over pears and smooth the top.

Place pan in preheated oven and bake for 50–60 minutes, until cake feels firm to the touch and starts to pull away from sides of pan. Remove from oven and leave to cool for a few minutes. Release sides of cake pan and invert cake onto a cooling rack.

Serve with warm or at room temperature, with double cream.

serves 8–10

Poach pears up to 2 days ahead. Cake is best made on the day.

poached summer fruits

6 small white peaches

6 nectarines

6 apricots

6 plums

4 cups water

450 g sugar

1 cinnamon stick

zest of ½ orange

double cream and almond bread, to serve

Wash fruit well, remove any stems and score a small cross at the base of each piece of fruit.

Put water, sugar, cinnamon stick and orange zest in a large saucepan and bring to the boil, stirring until sugar is dissolved. Add fruit, reduce heat to very low and simmer for 10–15 minutes, until fruit is soft. The syrup will reduce and thicken.

Remove from heat, fish out cinnamon stick and allow syrup to cool. Cover and refrigerate until needed. Serve with double cream and almond bread.

serves 10–12

Poach fruit up to 3 days ahead; keep covered in fridge.

portuguese custard tarts

225 g caster sugar

½ cup water

25 g cornflour

2 cups milk

½ cup thickened cream

3 egg yolks, lightly beaten

3 sheets ready-rolled butter puff pastry

icing sugar, to serve (optional)

Place sugar and water in a medium-sized saucepan over medium–high heat. Cook, stirring, for 2–3 minutes or until sugar dissolves. Bring to boil and boil, without stirring, for 3 minutes.

Put cornflour in a bowl and gradually add milk, stirring until combined. Add cream and mix well. Add egg yolks and whisk, then add sugar syrup, whisking until combined. Pour mixture into a saucepan and cook over medium heat until custard comes to the boil. Remove from heat and set aside to cool.

Preheat oven to 220°C. Lightly oil a 12-hole, non-stick cupcake pan, or individual small tart pans.

Cut pastry into 12 × 8-cm rounds. Press pastry into pans, and prick bases with a fork. Spoon in cool custard, half-filling cases. Place on top shelf in preheated oven and bake for 15–20 minutes until pastry is golden. Some dark spots will appear on the pastry and custard as it cooks.

>

Remove tarts from oven, leave to cool in tray for a few minutes, then transfer to a cooling rack.

Serve warm or at room temperature. Dust with icing sugar if desired.

makes 12

Can be cooked 1 day ahead and reheated, but are best made and eaten on the same day.

spotty cupcakes

250 g self-raising flour

pinch of salt

225 g caster sugar

100 g butter, at room temperature

3 eggs

⅓ cup milk

1 teaspoon vanilla extract

PINK CHOCOLATE ICING

120 g white chocolate, chopped

140 g unsalted butter, at room temperature

140 g icing sugar, sifted

pink food colouring

ready-made white icing in a piping bag (available at some supermarkets and specialty food stores)

Preheat oven to 175°C. Line a mini-muffin pan with paper patty-pan cases.

Sift flour, salt and sugar into a bowl. Add butter, eggs, milk and vanilla extract, and beat with an electric mixer until light and creamy. Spoon mixture into pan, place in preheated oven and bake for 8–10 minutes. Cool on wire rack before icing.

To make icing, put chocolate in heatproof bowl over simmering water and stir until melted (don't let the bowl touch the water). Allow to cool.

>

Meanwhile, beat butter and icing sugar with an electric mixer until light and fluffy. Add the tiniest amount of the food colouring to make the icing a very delicate pink, then beat in the melted chocolate. Ice the cupcakes, then use the ready-made icing to pipe small spots onto each one.

makes about 30

Icing – make up to 5 days ahead. Cupcakes – make and ice up to 1 day ahead; store in airtight container in cool place, or cover and refrigerate.

white chocolate
semifreddo with berry salad

300 g white chocolate, broken into chunks

4 eggs, separated

300 ml cream

500–600 g mixed berries (e.g. strawberries,
raspberries, blueberries)

1 tablespoon caster sugar

Place white chocolate in a heatproof bowl over a pan of simmering
water (make sure the bottom of the bowl does not touch water). Stir until
chocolate is melted, then remove from heat and allow to cool a little. Add
egg yolks and whisk until combined.

Pour cream into a separate bowl and whisk until it forms soft peaks. Fold
whipped cream into the chocolate mixture.

Place egg whites in a clean, dry bowl and whisk until soft peaks form.
Fold into chocolate mixture and stir well to combine. Pour mixture into a
non-stick loaf or log pan. Place in freezer and freeze for at least 6 hours,
or overnight.

>

To make berry salad, carefully rinse fruit, place in a bowl, sprinkle with sugar, and toss gently together. Cover, and refrigerate until ready to serve.

To serve, remove semifreddo from freezer and invert onto a serving platter. Cut into slices and top with berry salad.

serves 6–8

Semifreddo – make up to 4 days ahead. Fruit salad – make up to 1 day ahead.

Extras

Whether you're having a few friends round for drinks or dishing up for a crowd, some classic dips and sauces are a boon. They can be used to eke things out — just accompany them with crudites or water biscuits — or as accompaniments to some of the delicious finger food you'll find in the 'small bites' section.

As with the catering generally, don't neglect the presentation. Bring out your best dishes, bowls and platters for extra impact.

< black-olive tapenade (page 210)

black-olive tapenade

1½ cups pitted black olives

1 clove garlic

½ cup capers, rinsed and drained

1 tablespoon freshly squeezed lemon juice

3 anchovy fillets, rinsed

freshly ground black pepper

½ cup olive oil

Place all ingredients, except the oil, in a blender or food processor, and blend to a paste. Gradually pour in the oil and blend again until combined – you can make it smooth or leave it a little chunky.

Serve spread on crostini, topped with a slice of fresh mozzarella and a basil leaf.

serves 6–8

⊗ Make up to a week ahead; refrigerate in airtight container.

classic mayonnaise

2 egg yolks
1 teaspoon Dijon mustard
1 tablespoon freshly squeezed lemon juice
1 cup olive oil
salt and freshly ground black pepper

Place egg yolks, mustard and 2 teaspoons lemon juice in blender or food processor, and blend until light and creamy. With motor still running, gradually add oil in a thin stream until mixture thickens.

Stir in remaining lemon juice, and season to taste.

variations

To 1 cup of mayonnaise, add the following and stir until well mixed:

- *harissa mayo* – 1 teaspoon harissa, or more if you like it fiery
- *mango mayo* – ½ cup fresh mango
- *roasted red capsicum mayo* – ⅓ cup roasted and peeled red capsicum
- *wasabi mayo* – 2 teaspoons (or more) wasabi paste

makes just over 1 cup

Make up to a week ahead; refrigerate covered.

eggplant dip with tahini

3 medium-sized eggplants

1 clove garlic, crushed

3–4 tablespoons freshly squeezed lemon juice

2 tablespoons tahini (see page 249)

½ cup Greek-style yoghurt

1 tablespoon virgin olive oil

pinch of ground paprika

salt and freshly ground black pepper

Preheat oven to 180°C .

Prick the eggplants with a fork, then grill over a gas flame for 5–10 minutes until skin is charred (this gives it a pungent smoky flavour). Then cut them in half, place on baking tray, flesh-side down, and bake in preheated oven for about 15 minutes, until quite soft. Allow to cool a little before scraping flesh into a bowl. Leave it to sit for 10 minutes, then drain away any excess liquid.

Mash eggplant flesh with a fork, then stir in the lemon juice, tahini, yoghurt and oil, and mix well. Add paprika and plenty of salt and pepper to taste. Perfect as part of an antipasto platter, served with small wedges of warmed flat bread, or with a platter of fresh summer vegetables.

makes about 2 cups

Make up to 2 days ahead and store in fridge..

hummus

1 × 400-g can chickpeas, drained
and rinsed

½ cup water

freshly squeezed juice
of 2 lemons

125 ml tahini (see page 249)

2 cloves garlic, crushed

½ teaspoon salt

½ teaspoon ground cumin

½ teaspoon ground cayenne

3 tablespoons olive oil

Place all the ingredients in a blender or processor and blend until
thick – you can leave it a little chunky or process to quite a smooth paste.
Taste for additional salt and lemon juice.

To serve, place in serving bowl, drizzle over a little oil and a scattering
of cayenne pepper. Serve as a dip with crudités (page 55), or toasted
French bread.

makes 1½ cups

Make 2–3 days ahead and keep refrigerated.

Freezes well.

lemon aioli

½ cup mayonnaise (page 211)
½ cup Greek-style yoghurt
1 tablespoon freshly squeezed lemon juice
½ teaspoon finely grated lemon zest
1 clove garlic, crushed

Mix all the ingredients together in a bowl, cover, and refrigerate until needed.

makes about 1 cup

Make up to 3 days ahead; refrigerate covered.

pesto

2 cups torn fresh basil leaves

2 cloves garlic, crushed

3 tablespoons toasted pine nuts

½ cup virgin olive oil

½ cup freshly grated parmesan cheese

salt and freshly ground black pepper

Place basil leaves and garlic in a blender or food processor and process until well crushed. Add pine nuts, then gradually add oil and keep pulsing until you have a chunky paste.

Stir in the grated parmesan and season with salt and pepper to taste (don't overdo it, as the flavours take a little while to develop).

variations

Substitute different herbs and nuts (e.g. use rocket & hazelnuts; mint, parsley & pine nuts; or coriander & walnuts) then follow the instructions as above.

makes about 1 cup

Make up to 1 week ahead; store in fridge in airtight container. To keep longer, pour a layer of olive oil on top before sealing.

purée of cannellini beans

2 x 400-g cannellini beans, rinsed and drained

3 cloves garlic, crushed

2 tablespoons freshly squeezed lemon juice, or to taste

3–4 tablespoons olive oil

salt and freshly ground black pepper

generous pinch of ground paprika

about 2 tablespoons finely chopped fresh flat-leaf parsley

Place the beans, garlic, lemon juice and olive oil in a food processor and pulse to a coarse purée. Season with salt and pepper, and add more oil or lemon juice to taste if mixture is too thick.

Serve on plates or in bowls, sprinkled with paprika and parsley. A great quick extra, accompanied by pita wedges.

makes 2–3 cups

Make 1 day ahead; store in fridge, covered with plastic wrap.

sweet tomato chutney

2 tablespoons virgin olive oil

2 shallots or pickling onions, finely sliced

1 clove garlic, finely chopped

½ tablespoon ground coriander

½ teaspoon ground cumin

1.5 kg tomatoes, peeled, seeded and chopped

½ tablespoons grated fresh ginger

¼ cup brown sugar

¼ cup red wine vinegar

salt and freshly ground black pepper

Heat oil in a large saucepan over medium heat and cook onions for 5 minutes, or until soft. Add garlic and cook for 1 minute. Stir in coriander and cumin, and cook for 1–2 minutes or until fragrant. Add chopped tomatoes, ginger, sugar and vinegar and stir well.

Partially cover pan and simmer gently for 1–1½ hours, stirring occasionally, until chutney is thick. Season to taste with salt and pepper.

When completely cool, pour into a clean airtight jar. Store in fridge as an alternative accompaniment for finger food such as mini sausage rolls (page 88) or keftedes (page 79).

makes 1½ cups

catering for a crowd

If the occasion calls for a more substantial meal, consider serving one or two varieties of 'small bites' to start and then provide a buffet-style meal.

Buffet dishes need to be large and generous, and laid out so that guests can put together their own combinations. Keep it simple but stylish.

Provide plenty of good-quality bread, stack up the plates, polish up the silver, pile up the napkins and leave your guests to it. It also means less work for you (at least while the party is under way).

The recipes in this section are also appropriate for a sit-down dinner, and in most cases the quantities can easily be doubled. A dish that will serve 6 at a dinner will usually serve 8–10 as part of a buffet, as guests tend to choose smaller portions from more dishes.

For some sweet dishes suitable for larger-scale parties, see the 'sweet bites' section.

< chicken stuffed with veal & pistachios (page 222)

chicken stuffed with veal & pistachios

1 tablespoon olive oil

1 red onion, chopped

1 clove garlic, crushed

3 slices stale bread

½ cup milk

400 g veal mince

⅓ cup chopped pistachios

¼ cup grated parmesan cheese

¼ teaspoon grated nutmeg

3 tablespoons finely chopped flat-leaf parsley

1 sprig fresh thyme, leaves chopped

salt and freshly ground black pepper

1 large chicken, boned (ask the butcher to do this), or 2–3 boned chicken breasts, flattened out

Preheat oven to 180°C.

To make stuffing, heat oil in a non-stick frying pan, add onion and garlic, and sauté for 2–3 minutes until soft and golden.

Soak bread in milk for a few minutes until soft, then drain and squeeze out excess liquid. Put veal mince, onion and garlic, bread, pistachios, parmesan, nutmeg, parsley and thyme in a bowl, season with salt and pepper to taste, and mix well.

Lay chicken flat, then spoon stuffing along centre from end to end. Roll chicken lengthways firmly to form a log. Tie with kitchen string in several places to keep stuffing in place. Season outside of chicken with salt and pepper, place in a non-stick baking tray and drizzle with the remaining olive oil. Place in preheated oven and roast for 1 hour. If it is cooked, juices will run clear when pierced with a skewer.

Allow to cool a little, then remove string and cut roll into slices. Arrange on a platter and serve hot, or cold.

serves 6–8

Prepare up to 3 days ahead; store uncooked in fridge and return to room temperature before cooking. Or cook up to 3 days ahead and keep in fridge; serve cold.

chickpea & fresh herb salad

2 × 400-g cans chickpeas, drained and rinsed

1 clove garlic, crushed

2 spring onions, chopped

2 tablespoons chopped flat-leaf parsley

1 tablespoon chopped fresh mint

1 tablespoon chopped fresh oregano

½ teaspoon ras el hanout (see page 249)

freshly ground black pepper

ground sweet paprika, to serve (optional)

DRESSING

2 tablespoons Dijonnaise (see page 248)

1 tablespoon extra-virgin olive oil

1 tablespoon freshly squeezed lemon juice

Put all non-dressing ingredients in a large bowl and mix to combine.

To make the dressing, combine Dijonnaise, oil and lemon juice, then pour over salad and toss until chickpeas are coated. Cover and leave for at least 30 minutes for flavours to develop. Serve with a fine dusting of paprika on top if desired.

serves 8 as part of a buffet

Make up to 2 days ahead.

honey-ginger glazed ham

½ cured ham on the bone

25 cloves

2 cups boiling water

GLAZE

¾ cup honey

¼ cup bitter orange marmalade

¼ cup freshly squeezed orange juice

2 tablespoons soy sauce

2 tablespoons grated fresh ginger

1 tablespoon Dijon mustard

To make glaze, place all ingredients in a small saucepan over medium heat, stir to combine and simmer for about 5 minutes. Allow to cool. You can leave this overnight for the flavours to develop if you like.

Preheat oven to 175°C.

Carefully remove outer skin from ham, and use a sharp knife to cut a diamond pattern into the white fat. Place ham on a roasting rack in a baking pan. Brush with the glaze, then insert a clove into the centre of each diamond. Pour 2 cups of boiling water into baking pan.

Place pan in preheated oven and bake ham for 15 minutes. Brush with more glaze, then bake for a further 10 minutes. Remove from oven, cover with aluminium foil and leave for 10–15 minutes before carving.

You can serve the ham hot, warm or at room temperature.

serves 10–12 as part of a buffet

Bake ham up to 2 days ahead; store in fridge. Return to room temperature to serve. If serving ham hot or warm, bake it on the day.

mixed greens, herb & hazelnut salad

400 g mixed salad greens

½ cup fresh coriander leaves

½ cup fresh basil leaves

½ cup chopped chives

½ cups hazelnuts

DRESSING

1 tablespoon hazelnut oil

2 tablespoons virgin olive oil

1 tablespoon white balsamic vinegar

1 tablespoon cream

2 teaspoons Dijon mustard

salt and freshly ground black pepper

To make dressing, place all ingredients in a small bowl and whisk until combined. Cover and refrigerate until ready to use.

Preheat oven to 180°C. Line a baking tray with non-stick baking paper. Place hazelnuts on tray and roast for about 10 minutes. Remove from oven, rub off skins and roughly chop the nuts.

Wash and dry salad greens and herbs. Put in serving bowl and sprinkle hazelnuts over. Pour dressing over and toss salad immediately before serving.

serves 10–12 as part of a buffet

Dressing – make up to 2 days ahead (but add to salad just before serving); keep refrigerated. Salad leaves – prepare 1 day ahead; refrigerate covered. Nuts – roast up to 7 days ahead; keep in airtight container.

moroccan roast spatchcock

5 spatchcocks, cut into quarters

½ cup water

2 tablespoons fresh coriander leaves

harissa (see page 248) and Greek-style yoghurt, to serve

MARINADE

2 cloves garlic, crushed

1 long fresh red chilli, deseeded and finely sliced

¼ cup freshly squeezed lime juice

2 tablespoons chopped fresh coriander

1 teaspoon baharat (see page 248)

½ teaspoon ground fennel

2 tablespoons honey

2 tablespoons olive oil

salt and freshly ground black pepper

To make marinade, place all ingredients in a bowl and whisk until combined.

Place spatchcocks in one or two large shallow dishes, pour marinade over and turn until pieces are coated. Cover, and refrigerate for 3–4 hours or overnight.

Preheat oven to 220°C.

Place two roasting racks in two large baking dishes and pour ¼ cup water into the base of each dish. Place spatchcocks on racks, put in preheated oven and roast for about 40–45 minutes until cooked.

Arrange spatchcocks on a serving platter. Scatter with coriander leaves and serve with small bowl of spicy harissa and a bowl of thick yoghurt on the side.

serves 10

Marinate spatchcock up to 2 days ahead. Or marinate and cook 1 day ahead, refrigerate, and serve cold.

moussaka with roasted eggplant

3 tablespoons olive oil

2 onions, finely chopped

3 cloves garlic, crushed

1 kg lamb or beef mince

1 sprig fresh oregano

1 tablespoon chopped fresh basil

1 teaspoon ground cinnamon

½ cup chopped kalamata olives

1 × 425-g can chopped tomatoes

3 medium-sized eggplants, cut into 1-cm rounds

1 cup freshly grated parmesan cheese

1 cup fresh breadcrumbs

salt and freshly ground pepper

extra 2 tablespoons parmesan cheese

BÉCHAMEL SAUCE

2½ cups milk

½ onion, quartered

6 peppercorns

1 bay leaf

30 g unsalted butter

30 g plain flour

salt

2 eggs, lightly beaten

½ cup grated parmesan cheese

Heat 2 tablespoons of the oil in a large, heavy-based saucepan over medium heat. Add onion and garlic, and fry for a few minutes until softened. Add meat in batches and stir-fry until lightly browned. Add oregano, basil, cinnamon, olives, tomatoes and a good pinch of salt, and stir to combine.

Cover pan, reduce heat, and simmer for 30 minutes, stirring occasionally. Remove lid and simmer over very low heat for a further 30 minutes until mixtures thickens and reduces. Check for seasoning and add salt and pepper to taste. Remove oregano sprig.

Preheat oven to 240°C.

Cut eggplants into 1-cm rounds. Brush with oil, arrange in a single layer on a non-stick baking tray and bake for 15–20 minutes until golden-brown. Set aside, and reduce oven temperature to 180°C.

To make béchamel sauce, heat milk in a small saucepan with the onion, peppercorns and bay leaf, and simmer for a few minutes. Strain into a jug. Melt butter gently over medium–low heat, then add flour and cook, stirring, for 1–2 minutes. Gradually add infused milk and cook, stirring continuously, for 5–6 minutes, or until sauce thickens. Add salt to taste. Allow sauce to cool a little, then beat in eggs and cheese.

Lightly oil a deep baking dish about 30 cm × 20 cm. Place a layer of eggplant slices on base, then a layer of meat sauce, then some grated parmesan and breadcrumbs. Continue layering until all ingredients are used. Pour béchamel sauce over top, sprinkle with parmesan cheese, and bake in preheated oven for 45 minutes or until golden.

Leave to stand for 10 minutes before serving.

serves about 12 as part of a buffet

Cook up to 3 days ahead, and refrigerate; reheat, covered with foil, in preheated 180°C oven for 35–40 minutes. Or prepare to cooking stage up to 1 day ahead; refrigerate, then cook just before serving.

pistachio & pomegranate
couscous

500 g couscous

1 teaspoon ground cinnamon

1 tablespoon finely grated lemon zest

2 tablespoons olive oil

2 cups

2 tablespoons freshly squeezed lemon juice

100 g pistachios, chopped and lightly toasted

100 g fresh pomegranate seeds (or dried cranberries, soaked and drained)

3 tablespoons chopped flat-leaf parsley

3 tablespoons chopped fresh mint leaves

salt and freshly ground black pepper

edible gold leaf, to serve (optional)

Put couscous in a large bowl with cinnamon and lemon zest, and stir. Add 2 cups boiling water, 1 tablespoon oil and the lemon juice. Cover tightly and set aside for 15 minutes.

Once couscous has absorbed all the liquid, add the remainder of the oil and use a fork to fluff the grains.

Add remaining ingredients (except gold leaf) to the couscous and mix to combine. Pile into a large bowl or onto a serving platter and scatter with shreds of gold leaf before serving.

serves 8–10 as part of a buffet

Couscous can be made up to a day ahead and refrigerated, but is best made on day of serving. Bring back to room temperature and fluff with a fork before serving.

sugar-snap & snow peas
with toasted hazelnuts

500 g snow peas, topped and
tailed

250 g sugar-snap peas, topped
and tailed

1 cup toasted, chopped hazelnuts

2 tablespoons extra-virgin
olive oil

1 tablespoon hazelnut oil

freshly squeezed juice of 1 lemon

½ teaspoon ground cinnamon

To make dressing, mix all ingredients in a screwtop jar and shake until combined.

Steam or boil peas for 1–2 minutes, until bright green but still crisp. Dip into iced water to refresh, and drain well.

Arrange peas on a platter or in a shallow bowl. Pour dressing over and toss well. Add hazelnuts just before serving, and toss again.

serves 8–10 as part of a buffet

Peas – cook up to 1 day ahead; cover and refrigerate. Return to room temperature, and toss with dressing close to serving time.

tomato, mustard & fetta tart

2 large sheets ready-rolled
puff pastry

2 tablespoons grainy mustard

120 g fetta cheese

50 g ricotta cheese

100 g freshly grated parmesan
cheese

2 tablespoons chopped
fresh tarragon

salt and freshly ground
black pepper

1.5 kg vine-ripened tomatoes,
cored and thinly sliced

1 tablespoon extra-virgin olive oil

Preheat oven to 220°C. Line a baking tray with non-stick baking paper.

Cut two pastry circles 30 cm in diameter. Place one sheet on baking tray,
spread with mustard, then lay the second sheet on top and press lightly.

Mash fetta, ricotta, parmesan and chopped tarragon, and season with
salt and pepper. Spread cheese mixture onto the prepared pastry, leaving
a narrow border around the edge. Arrange tomato slices in overlapping
rings, then drizzle with olive oil.

Place tart in preheated oven and bake for 10 minutes. Reduce temperature
to 180°C and bake for a further 25 minutes, or until edges are puffed and
crisp.

>

Remove cooked tart from oven and allow to stand for 5–10 minutes before serving. It can be presented in slices or slivers, hot or at room temperature.

serves 8-10 as part of a buffet

Bake up to 2 days ahead; reheat, covered with foil, in preheated 180°C oven for about 20 minutes.

veal with creamy tuna & capers (vitello tonnato)

1.2 kg fillet of veal

salt and freshly ground black pepper

2 tablespoons virgin olive oil

2 cloves garlic, unpeeled

50 g butter

¼ cup white wine

¾ cup water

1 × 200-g can tuna in oil, drained

4 anchovies in oil, drained

3 tablespoons baby capers

1 tablespoon freshly squeezed lemon juice

1 cup mayonnaise (page 211)

1–2 tablespoons chicken stock

1 tablespoon finely chopped flat-leaf parsley

extra 2–3 tablespoons baby capers, to serve

Preheat oven to 220°C.

Season veal with salt and pepper. Heat oil in a large frying pan over medium–high heat and cook veal until browned on all sides. Transfer to a roasting pan, dot with butter and roast in preheated oven for 30–35 minutes, or until veal is cooked to medium-rare. Remove from oven, allow to cool, then cover and refrigerate.

To make the sauce, put tuna, anchovies, capers, lemon juice, mayonnaise and 1 tablespoon of chicken stock in a blender or food processor. Blend until creamy (sauce should be of pouring consistency – add a little extra

>

stock or water to thin if necessary). Stir through parsley, check for seasoning and add pepper to taste (the anchovies and capers usually provide enough salt).

To serve, cut veal into thin slices and arrange on a serving platter. Spoon tuna sauce over, and scatter with capers.

serves about 12 as part of a buffet

Cook veal and make sauce up to 2 days ahead. Assemble dish up to several hours before serving; keep refrigerated.

watermelon & fetta salad

4–5 Lebanese cucumbers

1 red onion, sliced as finely as possible

300 g fetta cheese, cut into cubes

1 kg watermelon, deseeded and cut into wedges

3 tablespoons fresh mint leaves

3 tablespoons extra-virgin olive oil

freshly ground black pepper

Trim cucumbers, cut in half and then into 3-cm chunks.

Arrange cucumbers, fetta, watermelon and olives on a platter. Drizzle with the oil, add a good grind of fresh pepper and scatter the mint leaves over.

serves 8–10 as part of a buffet

This salad is best made close to serving time.

whole poached coral trout

1 × 3-kg whole coral trout, cleaned

1 lemon, thickly sliced

2 sprigs fresh thyme

2 onions, quartered

2 sticks celery, thickly sliced

3 bay leaves

2 sprigs fresh parsley

1 star anise

1 tablespoon black peppercorns

200 ml white wine vinegar

1 tablespoon salt

Rinse fish well under cold water and pat dry. Stuff cavity with lemon slices and thyme. Tie once or twice with kitchen string to keep in place.

Put onion, celery, bay leaves, parsley, star anise, peppercorns and vinegar into fish kettle or saucepan large enough to hold the fish. Add enough water to cover, bring to the boil and simmer for 15 minutes. Add fish, cover, and simmer for 20 minutes.

Remove from heat and leave fish in water for 10–15 minutes to finish cooking. (To check, make a fine slit near the backbone – the flesh should come away and not be too pink.) Remove fish carefully to a plate. When cool enough, gently peel back skin.

Serve warm, chilled or at room temperature with a good-quality mayonnaise or hollandaise sauce.

serves 10–12

Poach trout up to 1 day ahead; refrigerate.

some special ingredients

baharat A Middle Eastern spice mix, available ready-made, with flavours of cumin, coriander, paprika, cloves, nutmeg and more.

chickpea flour (besan) Finely ground chickpeas, a common ingredient in Indian and Southeast Asian cooking. Available from Asian food stores, health-food shops and most supermarkets.

chilli jam Spicy, sweet–sour and sticky, this Asian-style sauce has garlic, chillies, cloves, onion and red peppers and often tamarind and dried shrimp.

Dijonnaise A creamy mixture of mayonnaise and Dijon mustard, available at most supermarkets. If you can't find it ready-made, you can substitute a mixture of equal parts Dijon mustard and good-quality mayonnaise (though it's not quite as delicious).

fontina An Italian cow's-milk cheese that is smooth and mellow when cooked. If you can't find it, try gouda or taleggio.

garam masala Indian spice mix traditionally including cinnamon, cumin, caraway, cloves, nutmeg and cardamom. Available at Asian food stores and supermarkets.

harissa A fiery Moroccan sauce of chilli, garlic and tomato paste, used in small quantities.

kataifi pastry A fine, shredded pastry used in Greek and Middle Eastern cooking. It can be used for sweet or savoury dishes.

kecap manis A dark, sweet–salty sauce used in Indonesian cooking; similar to soy sauce but thicker, sweeter and more complex in flavour. It is sweetened with palm sugar.

mascarpone A lightly whipped, soured, heavy cream, originally made in Italy.

mirin A sweet, clear-gold Japanese rice wine used (in relatively small quantities) for cooking.

nam pla (fish sauce) A salty, fermented Thai fish sauce.

nori Any of various Japanese seaweeds, usually sold dried or toasted, in sheets or flakes.

paneer A soft, cottage-style cheese used in Indian cooking. If you can't find paneer, you can substitute firm ricotta cheese.

panko breadcrumbs Japanese breadcrumbs that are lighter and flakier than traditional European-style breadcrumbs.

pomegranate molasses
A thick, dark, slightly sharp-tasting syrup made from pomegranates, used in Middle Eastern and Arab cooking.

ras el hanout The 'spice of the house', a special blend of roasted and ground herbs and spices, including cumin, coriander, turmeric, cinnamon and allspice, used in Moroccan cooking.

rice-paper sheets (banh trang)
Discs of rice batter, available from Asian food stores and some supermarkets. They are soaked before use, to soften them.

tahini A thick, nutty paste made from ground sesame seeds, widely used in Middle Eastern cooking.

tamari A rich, dark Japanese soy sauce that contains little or no wheat flour.

tikka paste An aromatic tandoori-style spice mixture used to marinate small pieces of meat, fish or poultry before grilling or baking. Available at supermarkets and Asian food stores.

wakame A delicate seaweed, typically used in Japanese cooking (e.g. in miso soup or noodle dishes). It is chiefly available dried, as fronds, flakes or a powder.

Conversions

OVEN TEMPERATURES

Celsius	Fahrenheit
150	300
180	360
190	375
200–230	400–450
250–260	475–500

CAKE-TIN SIZES

Centimetres	Inches
6 cm	2.5 in
7 cm	3 in
15 cm	6 in
18 cm	7 in
20 cm	8 in
23 cm	9 in
24 cm	9.5 in
25 cm	10 in
30 cm	12 in
33 cm	13 in
38 cm	15 in

LIQUIDS

Millilitres	Fluid ounces
60 ml	2 fl oz
125 ml	4 fl oz
200 ml	6 fl oz
250 ml	8 fl oz
500 ml	16 fl oz
625 ml	20 fl oz (1 pint)

WEIGHTS

Ounces	Grams
1 oz	30 g
2 oz	60 g
3 oz	90 g
4 oz	125 g
8 oz	250 g
12 oz	375 g
16 oz (1 lb)	500 g
2 lb	1 kg

Index

PENGUIN BOOKS

Published by the Penguin Group
Penguin Group (Australia)
250 Camberwell Road, Camberwell, Victoria 3124, Australia
(a division of Pearson Australia Group Pty Ltd)

New York Toronto London Dublin New Delhi Auckland Johannesburg

Penguin Books Ltd, Registered Offices: 80 Strand, London, WC2R 0RL, England

First published by Penguin Group (Australia), 2008

10 9 8 7 6 5 4 3 2 1

Text copyright © Penguin Group Australia 2008

Written by Margaret Barca

Cover and text design by Claire Tice © Penguin Group (Australia), 2008
Photography by Maikka Trupp
Styling by Lee Blaylock
Typeset in Grotesque MT by Post Pre-press Group, Brisbane, Queensland
Scanning and separations by Splitting Image, Clayton, Vic.
Printed in China by Everbest Printing Co. Ltd

Cataloguing information for this book is available from
the National Library of Australia

ISBN 978 0 14 300813 2

penguin.com.au